WITHDRAWN

INFORMAL "DIPLOMATIC RELATIONS"
The Case of Japan and the Republic of China, 1972-1974

By

David Nelson Rowe

Foreign Area Studies Publications

This is the fifteenth of a number of publications of the results of research carried on by faculty members and research scholars working at Yale University in the field of Foreign Area Studies. In 1953 there was published *The Multi-State System of Ancient China* by Richard A. Walker, and in 1954 there were published *The Russian Hexameter* by Richard T. Burgi and *China's March Toward the Tropics* by Herold J. Wiens. This was followed in 1960 by the *Index to Ch'ing Tai Ch'ou Pan I Wu Shih Mo* edited by David Nelson Rowe. In 1961 was published *Britain's Imperial Role in the Red Sea Area 1800-1878* by Thomas E. Marston, and *What China Policy?* by Vladimir Petrov. In 1964 there was published *United States Foreign Policy Toward South Africa 1948-1963* by Leon M. S. Slawecki, and in 1965, *Taiwan in China's Foreign Relations 1836-1874* by Sophia Su-fei Yen. In 1968 were published *The Opening of Korea: A Study in Chinese Diplomacy, 1876-1885* by Frederick Foo Chien, and *The Filipino Reaction to American Rule, 1901-1913* by Bonifacio S. Salamanca, and *New Nations: A Student Handbook* edited by David Nelson Rowe. In 1971 was published *French Policy Towards the Chinese in Madagascar* by Leon M. S. Slawecki, and in 1973 was published *The Politics of the Eighth Central Committee of the Communist Party of China* by Peter R. Moody Jr.

        David Nelson Rowe
        Professor of Political Science, Emeritus.

© Copyright 1975 by David Nelson Rowe. All rights reserved. No portion of this pamphlet may be reproduced without written permission from the author, except by a reviewer who may quote brief passages in connection with a review.

Copies may be purchased from:

The Shoe String Press, Inc.
995 Sherman Ave.
Hamden, Connecticut 06514

Manufactured in the United States of America

INFORMAL "DIPLOMATIC RELATIONS"
The Case of Japan and the Republic of China, 1972-1974

Beginning from 29 September 1972 Japan established diplomatic relations with the Chinese Communist government in Peking and simultaneously severed its relations with the Republic of China.

Previous to this Japan had carried on relations with the Republic of China in one form or another ever since the end of World War II during which the two nations had been enemies in war. Hostilities between the two had in fact begun much earlier, dating back to the Japanese military takeover of Manchuria from 1931. After that date, until Japan's surrender to the Allied Powers in 1945, Japan and the Republic of China had been engaged in almost continuous conflict. With the defeat and surrender of Japan, the government of the Republic of China (GROC) had been one of the occupying powers in Japan. As such, its policy toward Japan was stated as one of "reasonable generosity" instead of one of reprisal. (Statement of President Chiang Kai-shek, 21 May 1948, in *China Handbook 1951*, p. 129.) Accordingly, all Japanese troops had been repatriated from China, and the Chinese government did not demand any reparations from Japan for the countless lives and heavy and damaging economic losses inflicted by Japan's invasions of China over a period of some fourteen years.

Under the terms of the Japanese surrender, as had been previously specified in the communiques issued by Allied leaders at Cairo and confirmed by the terms of the Potsdam Proclamation of 26 July 1945, all territory which Japan had previously "stolen" from the Chinese, "such as Manchuria, Formosa [Taiwan], and the Pescadores," was to be "restored to the Republic of China." Accordingly, on 25 October 1945, after Japan's surrender, Taiwan was formally retroceded to the Republic of China after some fifty years in Japanese hands into which it had originally passed as a spoils of war in 1895. And although the Republic of China did not participate in the Peace Treaty of 1951 to which the United States and other powers were signatories, a separate treaty between the Republic of China and Japan was drawn up and came into effect 5 August 1952. Under its terms, it was recognized that "all treaties, conventions and agreements concluded before December 9, 1941 between Japan and China have become null and void as a consequence of the war." This would include the Treaty of Shimonoseki after the first Sino-Japanese War of 1895 under which Taiwan had been ceded to Japan, and would mean that since that cession was now become null and void, Taiwan had reverted to Chinese ownership. Thus was legally ratified and confirmed the retrocession of Taiwan to the Republic of China which in fact had taken place nearly seven years before.

When the Peace Treaty had been signed on 28 April 1952 an exchange of notes had been effected by which temporary diplomatic representation was set up by the two governments. (*China Handbook, 1953-54,* p. 167.) Soon after the coming into effect of the Treaty, diplomatic representatives with the rank of Ambassador were exchanged between the two countries, and the Chinese Consulates General at Yokohama and Osaka, Japan, which had been closed down since 1937 were reopened, together with the Consulate at Nagasaki.

Even prior to this, and under the Occupation of Japan in which the Republic of China participated, trade relations had been renewed. The takeover of the Chinese mainland by the Communists had occurred by 1949, and the government of the Republic of China had moved to Taiwan. Even with that rather small part of the total territory of China still under its control, the Nationalist government had by 1950 developed an annual two-way trade with Japan of about US$100 million. (For the Financial Agreement for Trade Between Taiwan and Occupied Japan, see *China Handbook 1951,* pp. 130-36.) In the then developed state of the economies of Japan and Taiwan it is natural that the exports from Taiwan to Japan were almost entirely agricultural products, with sugar alone accounting for US$29 million, and rice and fruits another US$8.15 million. Japan's chief export to Taiwan was fertilizer, US$13.75 million, with metals and machinery also bulking large.

By 1953 the Trade Plan between Japan and the Republic of China envisioned an annual two-way trade nearly 50% greater, at US$149 million. (*China Handbook 1953-54,* pp. 169-175.) Of the US$74.5 million exports from Taiwan, US$52.5 million was to be in sugar and rice. And as before, fertilizers, machinery and metals dominated Japan's exports to Taiwan with some US$33.9 million of the total of US$74.5 million planned in those categories.

At the same time, the government of the Republic of China engaged in a variety of magnanimous actions toward its former enemy, including consenting to clemency for a number of Japanese war criminals convicted by Chinese courts or by the International Military Tribunal for the Far East. It also facilitated the repatriation of stranded Japanese nationals from the China mainland. And there were a number of exchanges of visitors between the two countries, including both officials and civilians.

Above all, the trade and other economic relations between the two countries flourished. By 1964 the two-way trade was valued at US$280 million, and in 1965 it increased by 25% to US$350 million, to US$370 million in 1966 and to US$465 million in 1967. Of the total two-way trade in 1967, imports to Taiwan from Japan amounted to US$314.42 million, or 37.1% of all Taiwan's imports. This imbalance in favor of Japan was largely due to increased import of capital equipment financed by Japanese credits. (*China Yearbook 1968-69*, pp. 206-7.) This helped to lay the foundation for the rapid growth of industrialization in the Republic of China which has transformed her economy from that of an agricultural and raw materials producer, to that of a producer of increasingly sophisticated and capital-intensive industrial products, mainly for export. On 15 December 1967 a Third Annual Executive Arrangement for Japanese loans was concluded, and Japanese credits for US$34,808,500 were made available to the Republic of China for power development and other projects. In that same year 82 Japanese enterprises invested in Taiwan and 36 Japanese corporations entered into technical cooperation arrangements with Chinese companies. (*China Yearbook 1968-69*, p. 361.)

These material developments had been backstopped by a variety of organizational and institutional developments. For example, a Committee for the Promotion of Sino-Japanese Cooperation had been set up, and by October, 1967 it had held twelve Plenary Sessions attended by high-ranking governmental and political personnel on both sides. (*Ibid*, p. 360.) Visits back and forth by various dignitaries of both countries were frequent.

Seen from this perspective, the rather sudden shift in Japanese diplomatic relations away from the Republic of China on Taiwan and in favor of the Peking regime of the Chinese Communists was a severe shock to the GROC and the people on Taiwan. In January 1972 the Chinese Ambassador in Tokyo had met with the then Foreign Minister Takeo Fukuda who assured him that the "Taiwan Clause" contained in the joint communique of Prime Minister Sato and President Nixon of November 1969 remained valid. This refers to the statement by Sato in connection with the U.S.-Japan understanding on the reversion of Okinawa to Japanese control, reached in November 1969, that "it was important for the peace and security of the Far East that the United States should be in a position to carry out fully" its defense treaty obligations in the area. (*United States Foreign Policy 1969-1970,* Dept. of State Publication 8575, March 1971, p. 39.) He stated further that "the maintenance of peace and security in the Taiwan area was ... a most important factor for the security of Japan." This statement had been singled out by Chou En-lai, Premier of the Chinese Communist regime in Peking as proof of a Japanese commitment to support America's defense of Taiwan. (Emmerson, J. K. and Humphreys, L. A., *Will Japan Rearm?*, Washington, 1973, p. 76.) In fact, in a speech to the National Press Club in Washington in November 1969, Premier Sato had gone beyond the wording of the communique when he stated that an attack on Taiwan which caused American treaty commitments to be invoked would be "a threat to the peace and security of the Far East including Japan." (*Ibid.*)

Even in January 1972, Prime Minister Sato continued to state the central importance of the U.S. security commitments in the Far East, and although he indicated a belief that threats to the security of both Korea and Taiwan were diminishing, he still stated that "both Taiwan and the ROK are contained within the scope of the security treaty structure." (*Ibid.*, p. 77.) And in the same month the GROC took comfort from the assurance by former Prime Minister Nobusuke Kishi that "the relations between Japan and the Republic of China would remain close." (*China Yearbook 1972-73*, p. 24.)

But on 18 September 1972 the Japanese government sent a special envoy to Taipei to explain that the new Japanese Premier Kakuei Tanaka would move toward "normalization" of relations with Communist China. The envoy met with Vice President C. K. Yen, Foreign Minister Shen Chang-huan and Premier Chiang Ching-kuo. The Premier made a formal statement to the Japanese envoy, concluding with the following words:

> "... the collaboration between the present government of Japan and the Chinese Communists is a grave matter involving the national destiny of Japan and the future of the whole of Asia. It is to be hoped that Japanese statesmen will take the farsighted, long-term view in distinguishing friend from foe and advantage from disadvantage so as not to repeat the mistake of the Japanese militarists in

launching their war of aggression against China. If they do not do so, they will not only make another mistake of historic proportions and bring harm to the Chinese people, but will also sentence their own Japanese people to another destiny of disaster." (*Ibid.*, p. 25.)

When it learned that the Japanese Prime Minister would go to Peking, the Foreign Ministry in Taipei stated on 25 September 1972:

"Now that the Japanese Government is proceeding to hold talks with the Chinese Communists, this is clearly an act in violation of the Peace Treaty signed with the Government of the Republic of China and harmful to the relationship of cooperation between the two countries re-established since the end of the war.

The Government of the Republic of China is the only lawful government of China with the mandate from the Chinese people to exercise the sovereign rights over the whole of China, whereas the Chinese Communists who have imposed a reign of tyranny and enslavement over the Chinese people can in no way represent China.

Any agreement resulting from the forthcoming talks between the Japanese Government and the Chinese Communists shall be considered illegal and invalid." (*Ibid.*)

And on 29 September, immediately after the Japanese government established diplomatic relations with the Chinese Communists and severed relations with the Republic of China, the GROC issued this final statement:

"Prime Minister Kakuei Tanaka of Japan and the Chinese Communist rebel regime made public a Joint Statement establishing diplomatic relations between Japan and the Chinese Communists beginning from September 29, 1972. Furthermore, Japanese Foreign Minister Masayoshi Ohira announced that the Peace Treaty and the diplomatic relations between the Republic of China were henceforth terminated.

The Government of the Republic of China, in view of the perfidious actions of the Japanese Government in total disregard of treaty obligations, hereby declares its decision to sever diplomatic relations with the Japanese Government, and wishes to point out that the Japanese Government shall assume full responsibility for the rupture." (*Ibid.*, pp. 25-26.)

To put the actions of the Japanese government into some perspective, it is necessary to remember that although Japan had closely followed the policy toward both Peking and Taipei of the United States government, its real position in respect to China policy was greatly different from that of the United States. It had never followed a policy of completely isolating itself from the Chinese mainland regime, refusing to trade with it, or to have other and informal contacts. Furthermore, the sentiment inside Japan, particularly in the media and among the intelligentsia, had been strongly in favor of developing relationships with Communist China. Trade had never developed strongly, in contrast to the situation in regard to Taiwan, but even much more than in certain circles in the United States, there was always the illusion in Japan that some sort of huge potentiality for profitable economic relations did exist as far as Mainland China was concerned, no matter what the realities and problems of the present might be.

Thus when President Nixon radically changed the American approach to Chinese affairs, first by refraining from taking any steps that might have barred Red China out of the United Nations while negotiating with Peking for further U. S.-China Mainland contacts, and second by going to Peking himself while concealing this plan from even the Japanese who had loyally adhered to the policy of the United States in regard both to the United Nations seat of China, and to maintaining diplomatic ties with Taipei, the forces inside Japan pushing toward a *total* change in China policy were freed to help plunge the nation toward a *total* reversal of Japan's China policy.

It is only fair and just to say, that the primary cause of Japan's sudden and total change in this respect in 1972 was not only the dramatic reversal by President Nixon of the American policy, but its being done without even the slightest warning to the Japanese government. This is no justification of what the Japanese Government did, but it is something by way of an explanation.

The Japanese government, in fact, and the Japanese people, allowed themselves to be shocked into going much further than they needed to or had to. They not only got onto the bandwagon, but they put their foot on the gas pedal and pushed it down all the way!

Nevertheless, within less than three months after the breach of relations between Taipei and Tokyo, the two nations involved had decided that the substantive interests that lay between them, and the future of those interests and concerns, compelled them to develop some sort of means by which they would be able to conduct the business that they had to conduct, even though the "normal" diplomatic agencies and instrumentalities they had previously used for those purposes were no longer available to them.

Not only were there the growing Japanese investments in Taiwan, and the growing trade with Taiwan in which Japan enjoyed a handsome profit in terms of balance of trade. In addition, it was becoming increasingly clear that as we have it in American slang, "You ain't seen nothing yet," as to future potential in economic relations between the two countries, both growing rapidly. Taiwan was consistently reaching annual economic growth rates of ten percent or so. Everyone knew of Japan's phenomenal economic development. Could they agree simply to let such an economic potentiality go down the drain? Neither side could contemplate this.

In addition, there were other factors we have not yet outlined, but which did color the situation significantly. On the Chinese side, but no less a concern of the Japanese, was the presence in Japan of some 52,333 persons of Chinese ancestry and citizenship, as of December 1971, reduced to a figure of 45,107 by April 1973. (Reported by Association of East Asian Relations Tokyo Office, Section on Overseas Chinese Affairs, printed document, no date.) Perhaps half of these Chinese were of Taiwan origin and many of these had histories of long family residence and of long established businesses in Japan. The main concentrations were in the Tokyo-Yokohama and Osaka areas of Japan. Typically, throughout the vicissitudes of modern East Asian history and events related to China, they had maintained their Chinese identification and citizenship, and were overwhelmingly oriented toward the Republic of China even after the takeover of the Chinese mainland by the Communists after 1949. Also typical of the "Overseas Chinese" around the world, they were organized into associations, ranging downward from a United General Association of Overseas Chinese Resident in Japan with its office in Tokyo, to half a dozen major urban-centered Associations and some forty local Associations in cities and towns elsewhere. (United General Association of Overseas Chinese Resident in Japan, *Register of Offices of United General Association of Overseas Chinese Residents in Japan and of Local General Associations of Overseas Chinese,* n. p., August 1971.)

These Chinese in Japan represented quite different things to the different political governments and/or regimes concerned. To the GROC in Taiwan they represented a reservoir of political loyalty, economic affiliation and cultural identification of great importance because of their general economic prosperity and their strongly organized identification with the government in Taipei and the Kuomintang, the Nationalist Party. To the Chinese Communists they represented a focus of political warfare with the Taipei regime, to be won over by whatever combination of persuasion, threat or other inducement would prove effective. This was considered necessary in order to diminish wherever possible the influence outside of Taiwan of the Nationalist government based there. The aim of the Peking regime would therefore be to substitute among the Chinese in Japan loyalty to Peking instead of to Taipei, and to effect in all possible cases the political absorption of the Chinese in Japan by and to the Chinese Communist cause. Substantively this would mean that in all cases possible those Chinese resident in Japan should be caused to turn in their passports or other identity papers issued by the government in Taipei and to take out new identity papers issued by Peking.

To the Japanese government this Chinese minority was of concern mainly because of its possibly acting as an impediment in the way of complete "normalization" of Japan's relations with Peking, through its possible function as a preserver of Taipei's influence in Japan both politically and economically. It was no doubt the view of the Japanese government, as would be logical in light of past history, that whatever did happen to the political loyalties of the Chinese community in Japan, it would remain Chinese. The tenacity of the Chinese living abroad in preserving their Chinese character is too well known to merit discussion here. Suffice it to say that this cultural and political identification with China has been strengthened and supported by Chinese living abroad not only by the need frequently felt for mutual cooperation and protection, but by the constant and unchanging Chinese governmental concept of citizenship as based upon the *lex sanguinis,* or of ethnic origin. This has been the unvarying legal definition of citizenship by all Chinese governments during modern times when citizenship became an issue due to Chinese migration abroad and foreign residence on Chinese territory. It is reflected in the representation of Chinese living abroad in Chinese legislative and other governmental bodies, by corresponding Chinese political and party activities among Chinese living outside Chinese territory, and above all by the careful persistence of those Chinese in maintaining their cultural and social "Chineseness." For example, a motto painted in large black Chinese characters on the wall of the Chinese school in Tokyo states: "Chinese people will (or must) speak Chinese." (October 1973.)

To be sure, there was no such corresponding problem for either
Tokyo or Taipei in the shape of any very large Japanese community
permanently residing in Taiwan. The large numbers of Japanese who
had come to live there during the fifty years of Japanese ownership
of the territory had almost all been repatriated after the retrocession
of the island to the Republic of China in 1945. Some few no doubt
had blended into the native population of Taiwan and remained behind,
but not many escaped the careful scrutiny of the Chinese government
authorities charged with the repatriation task. It is nevertheless important
to note that during its fifty-year occupation of Taiwan, the Japanese
government had made powerful efforts at the cultural Japanization of
the Chinese population, with success as far as teaching the local people
the Japanese language was concerned.

The Taiwan Chinese at the time of the Japanese takeover in 1895
were mostly migrants from neighboring areas of the Chinese mainland,
mostly from Fukien Province. They came from an area of China in
which there was a profusion of Chinese dialects many of which were so
different from each other that they were entirely mutually non-understandable. To know more than one dialect was, in many areas, a simple
necessity of ordinary life. But one never failed to identify himself with
his mother dialect, that which was learned first from parents and other
relatives. Perhaps because of this historical situation in which many if
not most Chinese migrants to Taiwan had lived in ages past, they seem
to have a natural ease in the learning of languages. Thus, under the
Japanese, most of the Taiwan Chinese spoke at least three languages:
the mother dialect, at least one other Chinese dialect, and Japanese which
they had to learn in order to get along with their new rulers.

Even today after nearly thirty years under a new Chinese government
which has introduced universal compulsory education in the Mandarin
dialect of Chinese, the local dialects of the Taiwan Chinese migrants
and descendants are the ordinary languages of the Taiwan Chinese.
But Japanese persists also, particularly among older people, and enough
of its use persists among the younger people that there is a fairly good
ease of communication with Japanese visitors. This is a boon to the
Japanese, since they do not characteristically find it easy to learn foreign
languages. And this has meant that in increasing numbers Japanese find
Taiwan a good place in which to visit as tourists.

In recent years, what with increasingly rapid and comfortable air
transportation, thousands upon thousands of Japanese tourists have
visited Taiwan. Here they have found no problem of communication

with the local people, a problem that often bedevils Japanese tourists in other parts of the world. Also they have found that the local people in Taiwan, from fifty years previous experience, know what they want and how to get along with them and provide for their particular preferences in food, accommodation and other facilities. For these things the Japanese, with their increasing prosperity, now have the means to pay and pay well.

Lest it be thought that this heavy tourist influx to Taiwan from Japan is mostly profitable to the economy of Taiwan, we will be reminded that, as usual, the Japanese travels Japanese whenever he can. Thus the annual *profit* from Japan Air Lines flights between Japan and Taiwan recently amounted to no less than US$30 million. This made it the second most profitable flight sector in the JAL system, the single most profitable sector being that of JAL flights between Japan and Hawaii.

Here, in other words, was another very material area of interest between Japan and the Republic of China which neither government would desire to see harmed, in spite of the termination of the diplomatic relations between them.

Accordingly, and for many reasons in a large complex of interests, the Japanese and Chinese governments in Tokyo and Taipei decided quite quickly after terminating their formal diplomatic relations, to set up some kind of a system for conducting their business between them in the absence of normal inter-governmental agencies and instrumentalities for doing so. In less than three months this was done.

The first step was for each country to set up an organization on its own side. The Japanese set up the Inter-change Association (ICA) and the Republic of China unit was named the East Asia Relations Association (EARA). (Chang, T. K., "The Private Agreement Between Associations of the Republic of China and Japan Respecting Continuation of Economic Ties," *Asian Outlook,* Feb. 1973, p. 28.) Both these organizations were manned by former foreign diplomatic service veterans for the most part. On 26 December 1972 representatives of these two new organizations met in Taipei and signed an agreement to establish offices in each other's countries and to carry on relevant business there. (For full text of the Agreement, see Appendix, hereto.) In these proceedings the East Asian Relations Association of the Republic of China was represented by Chang Yen-tien and Koo Chen-fu, and the Japanese Inter-Change Association was represented by Teizo Horikoshi and Osamu

Itagaki. Mr. Chang is Chairman of Taiwan Sugar Corporation, a government corporation, and also Professor of National Taiwan University. He had graduated from National Peking University and had also attended the Graduate School of Tokyo Imperial University. He has had a long and distinguished career, mostly in the field of Agricultural Economics. His fluency in the Japanese language was no doubt a factor in his choice for this assignment. Mr. Koo, who was born in Taiwan and graduated in Law from the Taihoku (Taipei) Imperial University while Taiwan was held by Japan, is President of the Taiwan Cement Corporation, a government corporation, and is involved in a variety of high-level business and financial enterprises. He is, of course, fluent in Japanese.

On the Japanese side the signers, Messrs. Horikoshi and Itagaki, were, respectively, Vice President of Keidanren, the Japanese Federation of Economic Organizations and Board Chairman of ICA; and former Ambassador to the Republic of China, President of ICA. (*News from China,* 27 Dec. 1972.)

The Agreement signed on 26 Dec. 1972 provides that the two organizations shall:

1. Protect the interests of the nationals and corporations of each party residing in the other;
2. Handle what would normally be consular affairs relative to entry and re-entry of each other's nationals; etc.;
3. Provide assistance in the economic, trade and tourist exchange between the two countries;
4. Protect each other's fishing boats on the high seas off the coastal waters of the two countries;
5. Handle investment and matters pertaining to technical cooperation between the two countries;
6. Assist and cooperate in facilitating the air and sea transportation between the two countries; and
7. Cooperate in respect to academic, cultural and sports exchanges between the two countries.

In order to carry out these activities, the two organizations agreed to establish their respective offices in each other's territory as follows:

1. The EARA to establish an office in Tokyo and another in Osaka, the latter office being authorized to set up a branch office in Fukuoka, sending personnel there on long-term duty assignments;

2. The ICA may establish offices in Taipei and Kaohsiung.
3. The organizations may not employ more than thirty persons in their offices in each other's territory, but this is exclusive of local personnel.

It was further provided in the Agreement that:

"The two parties shall make sure that the necessary support, assistance and facilities, as their respective laws and regulations permit, be extended to the offices and personnel of each other."

This provision is quite general. What, in fact, would be necessary in order to make possible some effective representation by such organizations working in the territory of the other? Since the individuals working for them are, in effect, working for private organizations in foreign territory, are they to be subject, like other foreign nationals, to the domestic law of the host country? If so, they might be severely handicapped in the performance of their work. For example, in case the Chinese office of EARA in Tokyo were to deny a visa to a Japanese citizen desiring entry into the Republic of China, could that Japanese citizen enter suit in a court of law to compel EARA to give him the visa? This would create an impossible situation for the Chinese organization in Japan.

To ask another question with possible highly complicated implications, how could these private organizations carry on their work without some guarantee of the privacy of their communications with their home countries? This problem would be sure to arise, for example, in connection with the negotiation between the two countries of any more than usually complicated matter which might arise in respect to any of the areas of concern to the two organizations.

Another question bound to arise in the absence of prior agreement would be that of the status of permanent residents of either country in the territory of the other. Would their passports issued by one country, be considered valid for anything more than mere temporary travel status?

None of these matters, or numerous others in the area of practical operations, were dealt with in the Agreement. (See Appendix for full text.) In their absence from the Agreement it is logical to conclude that some informal and unpublished agreements must exist to take care of these and other concerns of both organizations and their respective countries. These agreements may be assumed to provide as follows, for

both organizations and their personnel in each other's territory:
1. Personal security of representatives of these organizations in the territory of the other is guaranteed by the governments of these two countries, including immunity from arrest or legal process arising from the "normal" conduct of the business of the organization;
2. Coded communications between the organizations in each country and their respective home organization headquarters are allowed, and documents not subject to postal regulations or intermediate inspections or surveillances may be transmitted by what would be the equivalent under normal circumstances, of a diplomatic pouch, in this case, however, handled directly by airline employees and not by couriers;
3. Overseas Chinese permanently residing in Japan and holding Republic of China passports may have the same privileges as before as to living status, organizational institutions and cultural autonomy, to include the security of their properties, schools and associations, in spite of the fact that their Republic of China passports no longer enjoy legal validity as issued by a "recognized" state. The same privileges would be enjoyed by permanent residents from Japan in the Republic of China;
4. Postal, telegraphic and telephone communications between the two countries would be maintained as previous to the rupture of diplomatic relations.

To repeat, none of these provisos are to be found in the Agreement, but they must be assumed to have been agreed to informally, for otherwise very serious obstructions could arise to prevent implementation of the Agreement even in its general terms. The obvious reason for not expressing any such possible arrangements in the Agreement is that the Chinese Communist regime could challenge their legality if formally expressed in an agreement signed by authorized representatives even of private organizations. Such a challenge might well be based upon the assertion that Japan, for example, was thereby providing what amounted to diplomatic privileges to the organization and staff members from Taiwan, said privileges rightfully inhering only to a regularly recognized national entity to which diplomatic recognition as such had been given by Japan.

In fact, there would be no way in which, if, in fact such privileges and operational facilities were granted to the Organization from Taiwan in Japan, the Chinese Communists could be prevented from taking some sort of action against the possession of said privileges by the members of the EARA. It is possible, that if such privileges could be proven to exist for EARA in Japan, that the Chinese Communist diplomatic establishment in Japan could in the future, and as they choose, move to secure their abrogation by the Japanese. We could expect, also, that any such movement by the Chinese Communists in Japan would proceed at a very deliberate pace, and would take up the matters involved one by one over time. This would maximize the impact of what would, indeed, become a matter of political warfare of the Chinese Communists in Japan against the Chinese from the Republic of China in Taiwan. We shall have to wait for developments of this sort to appear. But we will see, below, that very significant beginnings of a Chinese Communist attack against the *modus vivendi* between Tokyo and Taipei have already taken place, to the painful and costly loss on the part of both Japan and Republic of China.

But before we go on to these matters, there are a number of other organizational features with which we must deal. The Chinese in Taipei and the Japanese, as we have seen, had set up their respective organizations in their own countries before agreeing to the terms of their operations in each other's countries.

In Taipei, the EARA had been set up with Chang Yen-tien as Secretary-General and Koo Chen-fu as Under-Secretary-General. There was a Secretariat staff of thirty-four, divided into four sections as follows:

1. Secretariat for administration: 12 members.
2. Secretariat for Cultural and Information Work: 8 members.
3. Secretariat for Economic and Trade Affairs: 8 members.
4. Secretariat for Research: 6 members.

All the members of the Secretariat as well as the Secretary-General and Under-Secretary-General were fully fluent in written and spoken Japanese. They were either native Taiwan Chinese who had learned Japanese in the normal course of education under Japanese occupation of the island, or mainland Chinese educated in Japan. This language facility on the Chinese side was a great asset. But it allowed the Japanese side to staff its operations both in Japan and the Republic of China with non-Chinese-speakers, and to send its Chinese-language qualified personnel into the arena of their negotiations and diplomatic relations with the Chinese Communists.

For by contrast with the Chinese side, the Japanese operators in the arrangement were overwhelmingly not qualified in the Chinese language.

At first, the two sections of the EARA Secretariat charged with substantive matters in Culture and Information, and Economics and Trade, were not only largely derived from, but were strongly related to, the relevant sections of the Republic of China governmental apparatus dealing with such matters. Also, they were paid and their activities financed, directly by appropriations derived from the relevant areas of the GROC, such as the Government Information Office and the Ministries dealing with economic affairs. Thus had been duplicated, for the most part, the well-known situation of many governments faced with reconciling functional aspects of government with administrative arrangements and structures aiming at comprehensive integration and coordination of activities under various requirements. For example, is cultural and information work to be controlled by technicians in those fields who are experts, for example, in working in various media of communication? The answer is, of course, in the affirmative, but it is followed by a big "But," when the issue of the content of those communications relates, for example, to relations with other states. At that point the governmental organs primarily charged with responsibility for the direction and operation of foreign affairs, however multifarious and dispersed, will seek, and generally gain, control.

Thus the EARA in the Republic of China started out as a microcosm of the organizational and fiscal-support complexities of the major areas of government charged with the responsibilities for the various technical concerns involved in relations with Japan previous to the cessation of normal diplomatic relations.

But this was soon seen to be too cumbersome and awkward an arrangement, and the result was that EARA was given its own budget in the general budget of the GROC. For it had to be governmentally supported in spite of its "private" nature as an organization. Who else but government could or should support it, indeed? So we have the situation of a private non-governmental organization dependent for its financing upon the government from which in fact it was organizationally separate. It also derived its general administrative and specialized technical personnel from the government, but the personnel involved were simply separated formally from the government bureaus in which their careers had been centered. Some were given leave of absence, others were separated or retired. The variety and complexity of problems thus raised can be imagined.

For example, what of career foreign service officers thus temporarily given leave or separated? What provisions could be made for sustaining their career situations, involving advancement in rank, retirement provisions, etc.? Not very many persons were involved, but for those who were, the problems must have been initially dismaying. It must be recorded that no one in the EARA Secretariat in the Taipei office seemed to be under any pressures in his mind as to this. Nor did they allow the problems to demoralize them in any way. In fact, the office displayed an excellent morale, marked efficiency of operations and alert awareness of the problems of their work. This was clearly observable to the author in October, 1973.

As to the top direction of the EARA Taipei office, it might seem as though the Board Chairman, Mr. Chang Yen-tien, what with his Professorship at National Taiwan University and his headship of the very major government enterprise, the Taiwan Sugar Corporation, would probably not have adequate time and energy to devote to EARA. But this was observably clearly not the case. In every possible way he served as chief connection between EARA and the GROC. He had time and energy to devote even to the public relations aspect of his work for EARA as the author can testify. And as time went on he served very significantly in direct contact in negotiations between EARA and its Japanese counterpart in a variety of concerns. Like other top-level Chinese operators, the seven-day (and night) work week seemed normal to him, but he was also quite capable of relaxed participation in a friendly luncheon or dinner party with and for other interested persons. Of course he could rely upon Mr. Koo Chen-fu, the President of EARA to supervise the operation on a day-to-day basis. But Mr. Koo was also a man of many other responsibilities, any one of which a normal person would consider a fulltime job. Such are the multifarious talents, the seemingly inexhaustible energies and the assiduous devotion to public and civic concerns that characterize the managerial personnel resources of the Republic of China today.

Further, Mr. Wu Yu-liang, Secretary-General of EARA, was detached from the Ministry of Foreign Affairs of the GROC. A native of Tientsin, he had been educated in Japan where he had served nine years in three different diplomatic posts. During 1971-72 he had served as Director, Department of East Asian and Pacific Affairs in the Ministry of Foreign Affairs in Taipei, and as Director, Office of Consular Affairs there.

In Japan the main office of EARA was in Tokyo where it occupied three floors of an office building in a central location. Thus restricted in space, and limited very severely in personnel, it was heavily overburdened as to work load. The Representative there is Mr. Mah Soo-lay, born in Kiangsu and educated in Tokyo and Manila. He is member of the Legislative Yuan of the GROC and a member of the Central Committee of the Kuomintang, the Nationalist Party. He had had a distinguished career in journalism and at one time was President of the Board of Directors of the Broadcasting Company of China. Much of his experience was overseas, including Manila, Singapore and Djakarta, and he had also served as Advisor to the Chinese Mission to the General Assembly of the United Nations.

Under a Vice-Representative, his office was divided into five main sections: Secretariat, Economic Affairs, Cultural Affairs, Visa Section and Overseas Chinese Affairs section. The Research Section was under the Secretariat. The Information and Press work was under the Cultural section, as well as Education, Science and Cultural matters, together with the affairs of Chinese students resident in Japan. The section on Overseas Chinese affairs included three sub-sections, on general Overseas Chinese affairs, Overseas Chinese organizations, and Overseas Chinese Education, the latter dealing with educational concerns of the Chinese in Japan.

The Osaka Office is headed by Mr. Huang Hsin-pi, formerly a career member of the Foreign Service of Republic of China, a native of Taiwan, and fluent in Japanese. His office, much smaller than the main office in Tokyo, has four sections, a General Affairs Section, a Visa Section, and two others, one for Cultural Affairs and Economic Affairs, and the other for Overseas Chinese Affairs, and those of Chinese students resident in Japan. The Fukuoka office is a Branch Office of the Osaka Office. It is headed by Mr. Chen Chao-cheng, also from the career Foreign Service of the Republic of China, and, like Mr. Huang Hsin-pi, a native of Taiwan and fluent in Japanese. His staff is small, and his office is largely concerned with what would normally be consular services.

The totals of personnel in EARA in Japan offices are as follows:

1. Tokyo: 23 personnel from Republic of China; 30-40 local personnel.
2. Osaka: 5 personnel from Republic of China; 8 local personnel.
3. Fukuoka: 2 personnel from Republic of China; 5 local staff.

This brings the total authorized personnel from the Republic of China in compliance with the mutually-agreed-upon limit of thirty. It must be repeated again that this means a very heavily overworked staff, greatly

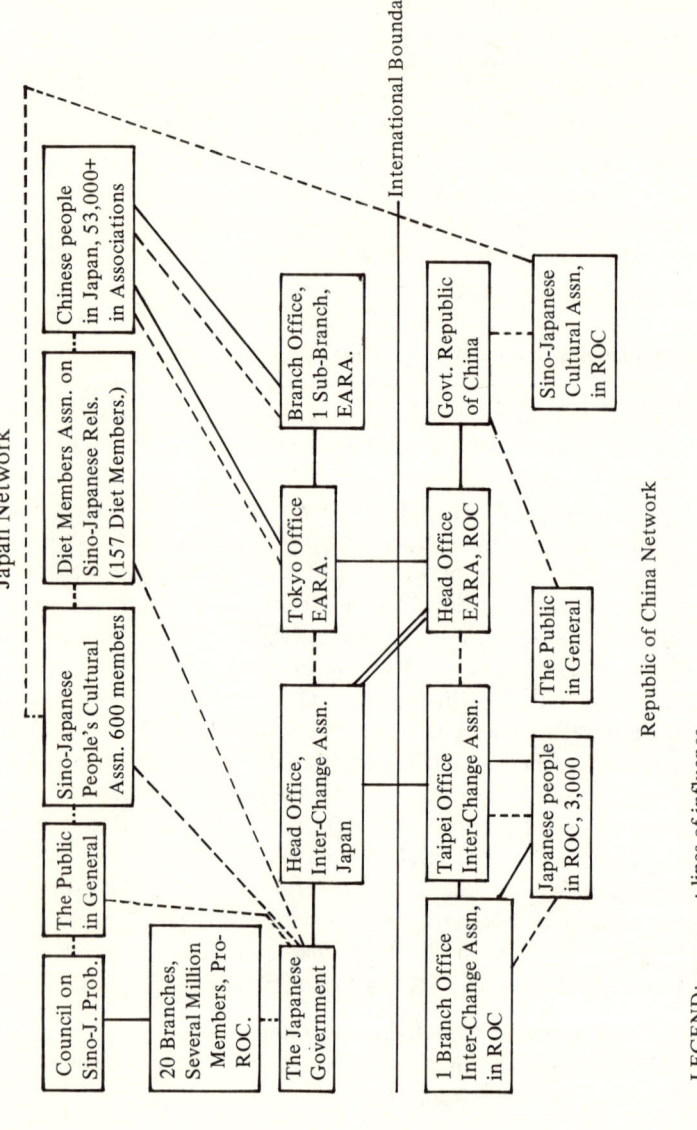

reduced below that of the former diplomatic representation but increasingly having more business to attend to than ever before.

But before we get into the conduct of actual business by the EARA in and with respect to Japan, let us look first at the actual network of communications in and between Tokyo and Taipei. The preceding diagram charts it out:

In reading this chart, it should first be noted that the vastly preponderant amount of daily and somewhat routine work was conducted by the Inter-Change Association of Japan and the East Asian Relations Association of Republic of China in their respective head or branch offices in Taiwan and Japan. This included such concerns as travel documents and identity documents of their citizens or citizens of third countries; economic and trade and transportation matters; cultural relations such as students from one country studying in the other, scientific and educational matters, and information work; and particularly for the EARA in Japan the individual and organizational concerns of citizens of one country living in the other. Some detailed consideration of these day-to-day duties of the two organizations will be provided below.

However, when it came to important policy matters, in particular, it became a matter for direct contacts between the heads of the two offices, in either Tokyo or Taipei, to discuss, negotiate and report back to their home offices which in turn would communicate back and forth with the home governments. And furthermore, in some very important cases, heads of these organizations would travel back and forth between the two countries, charged with representing points of view, transmitting positions on issues between the two countries and then again, reporting results of these contacts to their home governments directly. This frequently occurred, as shall be seen when we consider some of the issues that have arisen between Japan and Republic of China since the severance of their formal diplomatic relations in 1972.

Also, quite frequently it became necessary to supplement written or electronically transmitted messages from one association to its home office, by visits of the heads of the main association offices abroad, back to their capital cities. This would be particularly called for if and when matters of sufficient importance required complete guarantees of confidentiality of communications, since despatches or cables could no longer be assumed to enjoy even that degree of immunity from interception provided for by normal diplomatic safeguards. Since the distances and flying times between the two capitals are not great, a good deal of this sort of thing went on. But it did not preclude by any means visits by the Head Office Director-Generals to each other which were of course coordinated through the office chiefs in the capital city of the other country.

From the chart it will be noted that the Japanese organizations of a public nature concerned with Japan-ROC relations greatly outnumbered their Republic of China counterparts. This is natural in view of the fact that, so to speak, Japan at this stage of events represented a battleground of contending views as to China policy and by contrast the Republic of China constituted a more or less homogeneous opinion-area as to both China policy of Japan, and Republic of China policy toward Japan. Thus the Japanese who were interested and concerned with China policy matters and who favored the maintenance of close ties with Republic of China, although perhaps a minority of the Japanese people as a whole (and perhaps not), in view of the official policy of their government of rapidly developing closer and closer relations with Communist China, were impelled to organize themselves and work as hard as possible to uphold their point of view. It would be natural under these circumstances for the EARA in Japan to develop as close relations with such individuals and organizations as possible, but in fact this was most easily done through individual to individual contacts, both of EARA individuals and Chinese residents in Japan by and through their ever-present organizations. Cross-frontier contacts of organizations and individuals, such as between the Sino-Japanese Cultural Association in Taiwan and the Sino-Japanese People's Cultural Association in Japan were also useful here, but with some 53,000 Chinese resident in Japan against only about 3,000 Japanese in Taiwan, the Chinese had some assets and opportunities in this respect that the Japanese did not. Moreover, the Japanese in Taiwan had no visible or active opposition in Taiwan, whereas in Japan the Chinese Communist presence was not only visible, but forced a situation of more or less open psychological warfare and political warfare in Japan between the two sides. The Chinese Communists and the Chinese residents in Japan supportive of them were vastly outnumbered by the Chinese affiliated with and friendly to Republic of China. But they had facilities and recourses, because of their status as supportive to the Chinese state enjoying in Japan full recognition and diplomatic status, that the Chinese supportive of the Republic of China did not enjoy. Furthermore, whatever the nature and extent of the support for Republic of China in Japan among the public and within the government, there could be no doubt but that the official policy of downgrading and/or totally eliminating formal relations with the ROC was overwhelmingly supported in the media, among most upper-level intellectuals and generally throughout the educational system. Thus all those Japanese who supported for a variety of reasons the maintenance of all possible relationships with the Republic of China, and their Chinese friends in Japan, were constantly fighting what appeared to be a rear-guard action. This was increasingly the case as the internal party politics of Japan became seized of this issue, and, in particular, as the left-wing and the Communists and their direct and immediate supporters in the national legislature increased their representation in that body. The more the government policy went in favor of Communist China the more the left-wing seemed to gain in Japanese politics. And the more this happened, the more the government seemed tempted to try to head off defeat at the hands of the left wing by "going all the way" in its relations with Communist China.

What effect did this have on the some 53,000 Chinese resident in Japan? First, who were they, what was their general situation in Japan, and how did they react to the political warfare between the Peking and Taipei representations in Japan?

During the course of this study during the fall of 1972, the author enjoyed a large number of contacts with what are usually termed the "Overseas Chinese" in Japan, in Tokyo-Yokohama, Osaka and Fukuoka and surrounding areas. What is said here thus reflects a considerable number of conferences, interviews and discussions, as well as numerous social contacts with representatives of this group of people. Many of these people and their families had been in Japan a long time. Some had come over from the Chinese mainland in the 19th century, having been brought there by European traders based on the China coast to assist them in opening up trade with Japan. They made money at this, as they had when acting as middlemen in the China trade, and had in turn set up their own commercial enterprises. Others had migrated to Japan from Taiwan during the Japanese colonial tenure there and had stayed on. Some of these had, in fact, been among the numerous Taiwan Chinese who had served in the Japanese armed forces during World War II, of whom about 37,000 died in service. Others had gone to Japan after World War II, some from the China mainland, fewer from Taiwan. Among the latter were dissidents who used Japan as a sanctuary from which to organize and plot the overthrow of the Nationalist government and, they hoped, the establishment of an independent government in Taiwan under control of the Taiwan Chinese. The Japanese, it must be said, never seemed to inhibit in any way these dissident elements, which in more recent years have mostly fallen away, and in a number of cases reversed their previous opposition to the Chiang Kai-shek government and continually, to the present, have been received back in Taiwan by that government and not penalized for their previous actions.

In Japan, whatever their origins there, the Chinese residents developed a pattern quite familiar in light of their patterns of life elsewhere outside of China. They tended to live together, to set up "Chinatowns" wherever they were sufficiently numerous to dominate the areas in which they lived, and to engage in profitable commercial and trading enterprises. They educated their children in their own schools, and took care to see that they were taught the Chinese language and culture. Their ever-present "Hui" or associations served a variety of purposes, from legal aid, to charitable and "mutual aid" purposes, and generally provided mutual support to morale and some sort of shield against the overwhelming majority of non-Chinese among whom they lived and worked.

It is usual to view these Chinese "Hui" where seen outside China without remembering that they are no different at all from those found everywhere in China itself in traditional times, ranging from trade and craft guilds to religious organizations and groupings of fellow-provincials living in the "foreign" environment of another province. The local and particularistic basis of such organizations should not blind us to their potential for maximizing their membership and generalizing it geographically. In fact, these features, combined with a psychology at a minimum clannish and at a maximum secretive and even conspiratorial, had always directed the attention of traditional Chinese governments toward them as potential bases of political disaffection. With good reason was this so, as Dr. Sun Yat-sen demonstrated when he worked through them and established new forms of organization similar to theirs, in promoting the overthrow of the Manchu Dynasty with the support of the Overseas Chinese.

Seen from this perspective, it is no wonder that the political warfare between the Chinese Communists and the Chinese Nationalists in Japan focussed heavily upon the Overseas Chinese and their organizations. At first the Communists seemed to succeed fairly well. With the passive acquiescence of the Japanese authorities and their police, for instance, they simply physically stormed one of the two Chinese schools in the

Yokohama area and took it over for themselves. The other is still retained by the Nationalist sympathizers. Communist Chinese set out to win over top figures in the various "Hui," by a combination of persuasion and threat. About 3,000 Chinese turned in their passports issued by the Foreign Office in Taipei and exchanged them for Chinese Communist passports and/or identity documents. It would seem that a majority of these were persuaded that they could "do business" with Communist China, but that after trying, they were disillusioned. This could be expected, since, in line with their profit-oriented psychology, they hoped for normal commercial opportunities to develop with the Chinese mainland. But this was not to be so, since everything of this kind in Communist China was in the hands of government organs and agencies and existed solely for the profit and advantage of the state.

Of the 3,000, about half recanted, and of these, again about onehalf opted for Japanese citizenship. Of the total of about 53,000 Chinese in Japan, the Communists thus gained the allegiance of about 2.8%, hardly rewarding them for a lot of work. The author had an intensive interview with one of the more important Chinese who had been worked on very hard by the Communists to give up his identification with Republic of China and declare loyalty to Peking. He said they used mainly two arguments with him. First, they said, he should forget the past, come over to them and try to act as a bridge between the Republic of China and the Mao regime, to bring all Chinese together. The second main argument was somewhat out of harmony with the first, and was simply that he should join up with Peking and "commit himself to the motherland."

When asked why he did not accept these arguments he gave three answers:

1. The Communists are the only government in China's history that in twenty-five years has killed 60 million people of China;
2. The Communists are destroying traditional Chinese culture as seen in their attempts at language reform which will make it impossible for future generations to read the literature of the past;
3. "They never keep their promises."

He gave it as his opinion that the Chinese Communist regime is inherently unstable and must fall. He stated that those Chinese Communists who tried to win him over spent "many, many" hours in conversation with him, but finally abandoned their efforts. It is interesting to note that he would seem to have been a first class prospect for their efforts, since he had never had any strong ties to the government of the Republic of China either on the mainland or after its move to Taiwan, that he was of Taiwan Chinese extraction, and that in many, if not most ways he seemed to have been a notable case of Japanese acculturation. Nevertheless, he seemed, like many Chinese, to be comparatively lacking in any doctrinal or theoretical political orientation, and to be, on the other hand, of a highly pragmatic cast of mind, while thoroughly convinced of the superiority of Chinese traditional culture and at the same time completely adapted to commercial, financial and technological modernity. The predominance of this particular blend of cultural components in Taiwan under the Republic of China must have helped to account for his persistence in maintaining his relationship to its government, no matter how tenuous and removed that relationship might be. But as to this, it should not be forgotten that the "Overseas Chinese" are among the most persistent investors in capitalizing new business ventures in Taiwan today.

The persistence of the Overseas Chinese in Japan in preserving their cultural character as Chinese can best be seen in connection with their Chinese schools. The author had the opportunity to inspect closely the Chinese schools in Tokyo, Yokohama, and Osaka. In Tokyo this school was, as of October, 1974, the only place in the city still flying the national flag of the Republic of China. Under regulation of the Tokyo city educational authorities, its curriculum was entirely taught in the Chinese language, and went from first grade through six elementary grades, three grades of junior high school and three grades of senior high school. Not withstanding its being operated in the Chinese language it also taught Japanese and English, with Chinese and Japanese being taught from first grade on, and English beginning in the fifth grade of primary school.

There had been no rise in tuition charges for this privately operated school for three years, as of October, 1973. The Chairman of the Board of the School had argued that they could not increase the tuition without being accused by the Communists of operating only for the benefit of the rich "capitalists," so he planned to abolish tuition charges entirely and raise all costs of running the school through the various Chinese "Hui" in Tokyo. Presumably thereafter admission to the school, and retention in it of its students, would be on a competitive basis.

Originally established in 1929 as "The Tokyo Overseas Chinese School," it had suffered suspension of its activities during the war, and then resumed in 1946 under the name of "Tokyo Chinese School." The Principal, a native of Manchuria, had formerly been a Professor of Economics at a University in Taipei and has an impressive grasp of educational and administrative problems and a keen sense of public relations.

The textbook materials, while not those specifically put out by the Ministry of Education in Taipei for Overseas Chinese schools, were published in Taiwan by an independent publishing firm. The curriculum was well balanced and distributed, including languages, social sciences, physical sciences, fine arts, etc., with twenty-four hours of classes a week in first grade and ranging up to thirty-five hours a week in twelfth grade. The quality of the teachers and the discipline of the students seemed of very high quality. Every classroom was visited.

The impressions gained of this school were affirmed in the case of the other two schools similarly visited and inspected, those in Yokohama and Osaka. In all cases the buildings were modern and well maintained, the school administrators well trained and strongly motivated, and the schools well operated. Teachers seemed to have very good relationships to students and vice versa, and as always in these institutions, student discipline could leave nothing to be desired.

There is no question but that the attention given to Chinese residents in Japan by the quasi-official East Asian Relations Association of the Republic of China would have to be an essential in helping to sustain these institutions and their production of well-educated high school graduates, capable of going on to higher education in either Japanese institutions of higher learning or of attending colleges and universities in Taiwan. And as of June, 1972, there were some 10,000 Overseas Chinese students attending schools in Taiwan, of which 9,897 were from Asian countries and of which, again, 7,956 were attending colleges and universities in the Republic of China. (*China Yearbook 1972-73*, p. 413.) While the preponderant majority of those came from Southeast Asia including Hongkong and Macao, and the representation from Japan was small, this is to be expected since the 53,000 Overseas Chinese in Japan contrast with the total in Asia as a whole in 1972 of over 19 million. (*Ibid.*, p. 410.)

The Overseas Chinese students from Japan who would attend school in the ROC may be considered as an important element of intercultural relations between Japan and the Republic of China, since all or most of them would return to Japan to live and work the rest of their lives. In the cultural field, Sino-Japanese relations have a long history even in modern times. In the early years of the modern Chinese revolution, Japan, which led the way in modernization among east Asian countries, had been educating considerable numbers of Chinese youths who went back to serve their country's developing areas and concerns. It should be remembered, for example, that President Chiang Kai-shek himself had studied military science in Japan at the Tokyo Military Academy in 1907. A host of others who led the nation also were pioneers in the early days of Sino-Japanese cultural relations, by going to Japan for education.

The years of war between the two countries during 1931-45 of course ended this chapter in their cultural relations, at least for the time. But it must be remembered that traditionally the Japanese always acknowledged their immense debt to Chinese civilization, large elements of which they had absorbed and transformed, sometimes almost out of recognition. Seen in this way, the modern trend toward Chinese going to Japan for education was revolutionary, just as was so much else in the life of China then.

Japan's fifty-year rule of Taiwan was strictly on the colonial model under which almost all high-level jobs there were reserved to Japanese and the local Taiwan Chinese were almost completely barred from higher education with the exception of medicine, for which there was a demand for professional personnel the Japanese could not supply. With the end of the war in 1945 and the retrocession of Taiwan to the Republic of China, the Nationalist government was moved primarily by the need to re-absorb Taiwan into China, to revive and re-emphasize the Chinese cultural inheritance of the local people, and to this end to fight to destroy the cultural Japanization of the Taiwan people to which the Japanese had devoted so much energy for fifty years.

Accordingly, all publications in the Japanese language were banned from the island, and the use of Japanese in conversation was prohibited, although without too much success particularly in remote areas and among the older people who used it as a common language among the profusion of Chinese dialects in Taiwan. At the same time, the personnel who came over from the mainland took over the administration of affairs, not least to insure the rapid and complete reabsorption of Taiwan into the Chinese scheme of things, and rather serious and deep conflict ensued between the new arrivals and the people of the islands. This was accompanied by a policy of educating the young in the Chinese way, including the universal teaching of the Mandarin dialect, the National Language, in all schools at all levels.

Preoccupations such as these would naturally make difficult, if not impossible, any resumption of substantial intercultural relations between Japan, the recent enemy of China and colonial overlord of Taiwan, and the people there so recently come under the control of a government introduced among them from the Chinese mainland. But as time went on and the economic relations between Japan and Taiwan grew very substantially, the cultural interrelationship gradually renewed. As its political and governmental controls over Taiwan and its people gradually became firm, the GROC progressively relaxed its curbs on those wishing to go abroad, and this included students and other cultural personnel. The inhibitions against their going to Japan were still strong as a result of the war, and most of the youth wished to pursue their advanced studies in the United States or Europe. But some did go to Japan, perhaps a good deal fewer than should have, in view of the stronger relevance to the situation in Taiwan of much Japanese science and technology, by contrast with that of the United States, for instance. Thus at the time of the break in relations between Japan and the Republic of China in 1972, there were not a large number of Chinese students from Taiwan in Japan. A year later, for example, the whole area around Osaka, with a considerable number of educational institutions, had only about 150 advanced students from Taiwan studying there. There were no doubt greater numbers in the Tokyo or Kyoto areas. But the total was not large compared with educational centers in the West. The work of the East Asian Relations Association of the ROC in this field, while qualitatively important, was not quantitatively heavy. It took the form for the most part of liaison with the Chinese students' organizations in the various institutions and areas of concern. Osaka, for example, had five Chinese students' organizations for its only 150 student constituents. Thus these students demonstrated the same character of organizational proliferation as the bulk of the long-term or permanent Overseas Chinese in Japan.

As to economic affairs, the general state of Japan-ROC economic relations has already been described as of about 1967. But at the time when Japan broke relations with the GROC and entered into diplomatic relations with Communist China in September 1972, further very substantial development had taken place, much in favor of Japan as to trade, as the following table will show: (Chang, T. K., *op. cit.,* p. 29.) All figures in millions.

Year	Imports from Japan	Exports to Japan	Balance in favor of Japan
1968	US$423	US$152	US$271
1969	US$489	US$179	US$310
1970	US$582	US$235	US$347
1971	US$767	US$267	US$500

With a total two-way trade of US$1.034 billion between the two countries, for Japan meaning a favorable balance of trade of nearly half that amount, it would have seemed to imply great care, and a very gradual approach, to be applied to any policy of breaking mutual diplomatic relations. Also by the end of 1973 Japan had invested about US$100 million in Taiwan's economy, divided variously among about 404 cases involving about 534 technical cooperation projects in all. (*Ibid.*)

For the same years Japan's trade with mainland China was as follows:

1968	US$325	US$224	US$101
1969	US$391	US$243	US$148
1970	US$569	US$254	US$315
1971	US$577	US$322	US$255

These are far from insignificant amounts. It was, however, the feeling of seemingly large sectors of Japanese business and finance, that given the removal of political barriers in the shape of diplomatic relationships, the mainland China trade might be expanded largely, to assume in the future a size more in accord with the sheer size of mainland China with its population of some 700-800 millions by contrast with Taiwan with only some 14-15 million people. Similar ideas and concepts of the "potential" Chinese market have, however, dominated the minds of those in numerous places during much of modern history, in spite of which none of their expectations has ever really taken form. Given the restoration of order and integral civil rule on the Chinese mainland, it might well be argued, without too much wishful thinking, that the real potential of Chinese economic activity might be realized. But this has always, at least since 1949, flown in the face of the fact that under Mao Tse-tung economic development has always taken second place to political change, and that "normally" taking place by revolutionary methods. Furthermore, the Maoist political system places a very heavy priority upon economic self-sufficiency as over against any idea of expanding external economic relationships, the latter almost always being conceived, again, in terms of maximizing political objectives in and with respect to the other country or area involved.

As was anticipated, the rupture of diplomatic relations between Japan and the ROC did result initially in a drastic lowering of the level of economic relationships between the two countries. This can be seen from the figures on Japanese investments beginning in 1967 and running through 1972, the year of the rupture:

All monetary figures are in units of US$1,000:

Year	Cases of Japanese investment	Amount of Japanese investment in Taiwan
1967	76	15,947.
1968	96	14,855.
1969	75	17,379.
1970	51	28,530.
1971	18	12,400
1972	26	7,728

And the figures for approved projects of technical cooperation ran as follows: 1967: 41; 1968: 68; 1969: 72; 1970: 101; 1971: 79; and 1972: 36. (All the above figures supplied by Taipei Headquarters, EARA, October 1973.)

The same sort of trend developed in the all-important field of tourism, where the number of Japanese visitors to Taiwan dropped from 23,318 for September 1972 to 10,272 for October, the month after the rupture of diplomatic relations. This figure was 54.3% lower than that of the corresponding month of 1971. (Same source.)

It was clearly in the mutual interest for both Japan and the ROC to try to do something to arrest, and then if possible, to reverse these trends. But before we get into that, first let us examine carefully the Japanese organization, the Inter-Change Association, as we have looked at the ROC organization the East Asian Relations Association.

As would be expected from the Japanese government's emphasis upon strengthening all aspects of its relations with Communist China, the ICA in Japan has evidently taken on a low profile. Its offices are very modest in size, and the number of visible personnel sparse. Its Board Chairman, Mr. Teizo Horikoshi, does not seem involved in the daily operations of ICA in any significant way, the work being handled by the President, Mr. Osamu Itagaki, who is not only a former Japanese Ambassador to Taipei but has also occupied numerous other important Japanese diplomatic posts in various parts of the world including North America. This differs from the ROC pattern with EARA, where the first ranking official Mr. Chang Yen-tien, seems to carry a heavy load of duties in the organization. He, by contrast with Mr. Itagaki, is not a former diplomat of the ROC foreign service. But as already noted, his Secretary-General is highly experienced in Japanese Affairs, as well as in the general administration of Consular Affairs for the Ministry of Foreign Affairs of the ROC.

The contrast in respect to the main home offices, between EARA and ICA, is thus clear. The Chinese office in Taipei is larger but is headed by a "private" individual who has a major share in its most important work and who is not identified as formerly attached to his country's foreign service. Thus the "unofficial" character of EARA is emphasized, it not being until the third level down that an important official is found with strong ties to his country's diplomatic establishment, but who, on the other hand, although temporarily detached therefrom, must to all intents and purposes be clearly identified with it.

In the case of Japan, the home office of ICA is smaller. Its "private" individual head does not work actively in the day-to-day business of ICA, but leaves it to the Chairman, a retired high-level diplomat of the Japanese foreign service.

It is no reflection on the "correctness" legally of the approach of either country's organization to say that the Chinese of the ROC seem to emphasize size and importance of their organization as to its main office, while the Japanese deemphasize size and any importance that might be attached to it. The Chinese avoid very prominent positions for their own diplomatic personnel in the organization but at the same time place in the position of Secretary-General a career diplomat temporarily detached from the Foreign Ministry and who may as well be considered an active member of the diplomatic establishment. The Japanese pick a higher-ranking but retired diplomat, who while being effectively in the service of his country must from the purely legalistic point of view be considered as having returned to "private" life.

The only really critical observers of all this legal fiction are of course the Chinese Communists and their diplomats in Tokyo. How they evaluate the elaborate facades erected by the Republic of China and

Japan in respect of their activities with each other, is not known. The guess may be hazarded, however, that they fully appreciate the efforts of the ROC in making its home office big but "private," and those of the Japanese to make their home office unobtrusive but slightly less "private" since the Tokyo office of ICA is of course quite open to their scrutiny and they are known to be very sensitive on matters of protocol and prestige, and always weigh them from the point of view of political warfare.

By contrast with its Tokyo office, the ICA office in Taipei is larger and more visible. Headed by a Director, Mr. Horonori Ito, a former Deputy Chief of Mission in Japan's Embassy in Taipei just before it closed in 1972, he is now detached from the Japanese foreign service. His staff of ten, exclusive of local employees, includes only one person proficient in Chinese language. All others so qualified would seem to have been drawn off for service in connection with the opening of relations with Communist China. But most, probably all, of the local employees are qualified in both Japanese and Chinese, and so can handle the normal public contacts necessary to the work of the office. The office occupies an adequately large space in a modern office building in Taipei.

The Kaohsiung Branch office is headed by Mr. Shigehide Tanaka as Director. He is a detached Foreign Office official with a long diplomatic background in Chinese Affairs, including service on the China mainland before and after World War II. He has one other staff member from Japan and only three local employees.

Both these offices of ICA are organized into the several sections dealing with the various concerns of the two countries, including general secretariat, cultural affairs and resident nationals, management, visa and documentation and economic affairs and mutual cooperation. In a Chinese-language Press Release at the time of the establishment of ICA in Taipei it was stated in part: "In respect to the areas of economics and trade, the Taipei office is conducting the work done by the former Japanese Embassy in China." (Secured from Taipei ICA Office, October, 1973.) This is a clear statement of the facts in the matter, without any evasion or attempt to qualify. The Press Release makes it quite clear that this is to be the case as to all relevant areas of concern between the two countries.

As general back-up for these "informal" arrangements, the Japanese side began soon after the agreement of 26 December 1972, to develop several organizations of a public nature. (Some of these have been included in the organizational chart on p. 22.) In January 1973 Mr. Hidezo Inaba, head of OISCA-International (Organization for Industrial, Spiritual and Cultural Association) visited Taipei in connection with setting up a Chapter of his Organization in the ROC. (*News from China,* New York, 18 Jan. 1973.) A delegation of 116 Japanese visited Taiwan with Mr. Inaba, to attend the inauguration of the Chapter there. At a press conference Mr. Inaba said that Japan would continue to send technologists to Taiwan and to help Chinese specialists to acquire new techniques from Japan.

The Japanese leader said his country would provide scholarships for Chinese students and would continue its youth exchange program with the ROC. "We will also step up cultural and educational exchange," he said.

With headquarters in Tokyo, OISCA-International is a non-governmental Japanese organization with headquarters as of that date in Bangladesh, India, Indonesia, the Philippines, Singapore and Ceylon.

In April 1973 a new organization was set up, the Japan-China National Cultural Association, its President being an eminent Japanese historian of Tokyo University, Professor Uno Seiichi, a celebrated authority on Chinese classical studies. Two Executive Directors were chosen, novelist Fujishima Taisuke and Professor Kotani Hidejiro. They later visited Taipei in company with the Secretary General of the new Association, a Mr. Ito.

In the previous month more than 150 members of the Diet who were members of the majority Party in control of the government had organized the "Japan-Republic of China Dietmen Council," to support within the government the interests of the ROC. (*Ibid.*) Headed by Hirokichi Nadao, former Minister of Education in the Japanese Cabinet, the Council's main purpose is to support and promote the friendship between Japan and the Republic of China. It was established on 14 March 1973.

The first case in point which the Council concerned itself with was that of the disposition of the Embassy property of the GROC in Tokyo. When Japan broke relations with the ROC the government in Taipei placed its properties in Japan under the custody of the Japanese government on the condition that they would not be used, occupied or disposed of without prior consent of the government in Taipei. (*News from China,* 15 March 1973.) However, the Japanese government decided on 14 March to turn the properties over to the Chinese Communists.

The position of the GROC in Taipei was that it was the legal owner of the properties, which ownership had been registered with the Japanese authorities in accordance with Japanese law. Supporting this position, the Japan-Republic of China Dietmen Council cited the registration of the ownership of the property with the Ministry of Justice in Tokyo, and claimed that the matter involved a case under Japan's civil code and which could be settled only in a court of law, and not by fiat of the Cabinet and government of Japan. On 15 March 1973 representatives of the Dietmen's Council met with Prime Minister Kakuei Tanaka to protest the government's decision to award the property to the Peking representatives. In reply to their representations Prime Minister Tanaka said Japan could not step the Peking representatives from claiming the premises formerly occupied in Japan by the Nationalist government, and that there was no reason to refuse their claim to these properties, especially since the Japanese government was totally at a loss as to finding any other suitable place in which the Chinese from Peking could conduct their activities. (*China Post*, Taipei, 16 March 1973.) The Dietmen of Tanaka's Party were unable to effect any reconsideration of this matter by their Party head.

They also took the opportunity, however, of raising the issue of the air services between Japan and Taiwan which, in light of the Japanese government's efforts to negotiate an agreement with Peking for Japan-Mainland China air services on a reciprocal basis, were then coming into question. The Chinese Communists were making the continuation of existing air services between Japan and Taiwan an obstacle to any air services between Japan and the mainland.

According to the representatives of the Japan-Republic of China Dietmen Council who talked that day with Prime Minister Tanaka and Foreign Minister Ohira, the two Party Cabinet Members assured them that they would "try to retain the existing Japan-Taipei commercial air service." (*Ibid.*) This was in spite of the fact that the Peking regime had already let it be known that it would not tolerate having its aircraft parked in the same airport with airplanes bearing the flag of Nationalist China. This seemed to be an insurmountable obstacle in the way of getting a new air transport agreement with Peking while at the same time retaining the existing services of Japan Airlines and China Airlines of ROC between Japan and Taiwan. This position of Peking was a new one, without precedent during the whole time that, for example, ships based in Taiwan and the Chinese Mainland had been making use of port facilities in Yokohama and Kobe for ten or more years in the past, with neither Peking nor Taipei having made it an issue for protest or complaint in any way.

The real change, it would seem, was not in the area of Communist Chinese sensitivities, but in their comprehension as to Japanese aspirations. Prime Minister Tanaka, having "seized the ball" of relations with Red China, seemed determined to run as far and above all, as fast with it as he could. He was seemingly determined to outdistance the competition, particularly that of the United States, which, having initially "stolen a march" on Japan with the unheralded Nixon visit to Peking, could naturally be expected to push its advantage as far as it could. This was all only too easily perceivable to Peking, which thus gained new ground upon which to conduct its eternal war of political attrition against the Chiang Kai-shek "clique" as they prefer to term it.

But to attribute the Peking posture on this matter entirely to its desire to humiliate Taipei and reduce its international standing progressively as much as possible would be a first class error in judgment. The main objective of their political warfare in that part of the world was not Taiwan, but Japan itself. The aim was to demonstrate at every point, two fundamentals:

1. The political costs inside of Japan, which, with the willing help of the Tanaka government, they would demonstrate as consequent upon any opposition to the "leftward" trend of events in Japan itself by those whose political psychology had any ever so vestigal a character of anti-Communism;
2. The political gains which they would do everything possible in their power to demonstrate, would follow along after any leftward trend in Japanese political allegiances and alignments, as rewards to those who gave them what they wanted.

The ultimate objective of all their political struggle in, with and in respect to Japan was, is and will remain, the political takeover, at second or third hand if necessary, of that nation. As their logic went, the more political success and support to the ruling Party demonstrably followed substantive dealings of Japan's government with Communist China, the more the various factions in the ruling Party would be forced to orient themselves further and further to the left. Finally, they believe, the differences between the minority factions in the Party and the non-party leftists in the Diet, would tend to disappear, and the way would be prepared for amalgamation of those minority factions with the leftist factions in the Diet outside the ruling Party. This would gradually lead to a conglomeration of left-wing minorities in the Diet which, given time, could destroy the majority which the ruling Party had so long held, and finally the government of Japan would be entirely controlled by the left. This would lead to a virtual Chinese Communist takeover of Japan through the Diet majorities in the hands of the left. The objective of this was, of course, a fully intensive amalgamation of Japanese and mainland Chinese economic interests. This was the supreme goal of Maoist policy toward Japan. And the reason was not hard to see: given that type of political orientation, on the part of Japan, Communist China could then found its hopes for relatively rapid economic modernization upon a new form of the old "Greater East Asia Co-Prosperity Sphere," the dream of Imperial Japan before its defeat in World War II, but this time under the firm control of Peking, not of Tokyo. The alliance between Japanese technology, organization and discipline and energy, and China's people and resources, would then make China that major factor in world power that it could not become EXCEPT in some form of alliance with a source outside of itself for those assets it did not have and could not get any other way.

In the meantime, what was happening elsewhere in the spectrum of Japan-ROC relationships that had given rise to the December, 1972 agreement as to new organizations for carrying these relationships forward?

After the Agreement was signed on 26 December 1972, the EARA of the ROC opened for business in Tokyo on 4 January 1973. In the first three days thereafter it issued 1,000 visas for travel to Taiwan by Japanese and other foreign travellers. (*News from China,* 8 Jan. 1873.) And in the entire month of January 1973, 11,218 such visas were provided. (Chart provided by EARA Tokyo Office.) This number steadily increased to a peak of 15,369 in April 1973, fell off a bit to about 13,000 in May, and then went upward until it reached 16,943 in August and 16,840 in September, 1973. By contrast, the largest month in 1971, the last full year in which the Chinese Embassy in Tokyo had handled these matters, was April, with 7,438 visas being given.

It should be remembered in this connection that the Tokyo EARA office had very much less personnel and space within which to do all this work than the Embassy had had before.

At this point attention must be called to a technical device with which both the ROC and Japan offices successfully bypassed one of the most difficult potential problems to which attention was called previously in this paper. This was the problem of their legal liability as private organizations, for the consequences of their actions. What if, we asked before, any party applying for a visa were to be denied it? Under previous diplomatic immunity the Embassy or Consulate would be immune from any lawsuit in such connection. But neither EARA nor ICA, as private nongovernmental organizations, could plead such immunity.

Accordingly, both offices developed a system to avoid any such problem. In Japan, all ROC visas, for example, were given under authority of the nearest GROC diplomatic establishment, in Seoul, Republic of Korea, to which all applications were referred by telex, and from which permission was either granted (in overwhelmingly greater numbers) or withheld. Thus the local functionaries, in case of any protest backed by threats of legal consequences, could simply refer the applicants to the GROC diplomatic officers in Seoul who were not only far away and in another foreign country, but were immune from suit under normal diplomatic immunity.

In Taipei, the Japanese ICA did the same thing, by referring all applications to the Japanese Consulate General in Hongkong. But in their case, they stated, they actually sent the passports of applicants to Hongkong from either Taipei or Kaohsiung by pouch delivered to airline crew members by hand and subsequently transmitted to the Hongkong Consulate General and back by the same means. (Documentation from the ICA Taipei and Kaohsiung offices, to author, October 1973.) By contrast, in Tokyo, Osaka and Fukuoka, the EARA offices of the ROC possessed stamping apparatus derived from the Chinese Embassy in Seoul, which they used for the actual validation of the visas in the passports. This should suffice to do the job and at the same time avoid potentially embarrassing problems of legal liability. If, in fact, and there is no reason not to believe it, the Japanese ICA offices in Taiwan did in fact ship all passports to Hongkong for visa entries, they were perhaps taking an unnecessary precaution. It did, in fact, take longer to get a visa that way, for although passports were reportedly sent six days a week by air to Hongkong, the turnaround would take five days on the average, as reported in Taiwan by ICA. At any rate, the business load of the EARA in Japan was far greater than that of the ICA in Taiwan, due no doubt to the rather phenomenal growth of Japanese tourism in Taiwan. Although the number of Chinese from Taiwan travelling to Japan increased rather steadily, it never came anywhere near equalling the traffic of

Japanese to Taiwan. During the first eight months of 1973, for instance, after ICA's establishment in Taiwan, the number of visas and/or travel documents to non-Japanese travellers from Taiwan to Japan came to about 25,000, for a monthly average of somewhat over 3,000. (Documentation from ICA Taipei Office, Oct. 1973.) This compared with a total in the same eight-month period in the Tokyo EARA office *alone* of 115,716, for a monthly average of about 14,464, or about 4½ times the *total* Taiwan Japanese ICA load.

Ever since the retrocession of Taiwan to the Republic of China the government there had imposed strict controls over the foreign travel, let alone emigration, of Taiwan residents of any and all categories. Thus it safeguarded its supplies of foreign exchange and attempted to reduce problems of manpower loss particularly in critical fields. With increasing prosperity some relaxation in these controls has ensued, but they are still a constant factor, with the government trying to restrict such travel except when necessary. In addition, as Japanese prosperity has soared, the people have more money to spend abroad and can very often find their money goes much farther abroad than it does at home. This is particularly true in Taiwan, where even today, with inflation a difficult if not critical problem, the Japanese tourist finds all consumer costs considerably lower than at home. This has been particularly true of food and lodging, both of which in Taiwan are attractive not only in price, but in quality. Thus it is no surprise that in the period of three years 1970-73, over forty percent of all tourists visiting Taiwan were Japanese. In the last of these years, 1973, more than fifty percent of all tourists in Taiwan were Japanese. (*News from China,* New York, 30 Jan. 1974.) This was in spite of the feared reduction in tourist travel from Japan on account of the energy crisis of the latter half of 1973, which hit Japan extremely hard.

The importance of all this to Taiwan's economy can easily be seen. Whereas in 1972 total revenue from tourism in Taiwan came to US$128 million, in 1973 it increased to a total of US$210 million. (*Ibid.*) The only currently visible block to further growth in this sector is the shortage of hotel room space in Taiwan which even today badly needs about 1,000 more hotel rooms to take care of its guests. There is today a strict control of large high-rise construction in Taiwan due to materials shortages caused to a heavy extent by the considerable number of massive construction projects now under way for modernization of infrastructure and addition of new heavy industrial enterprises. There is no shortage of capital for hotel development, with several foreign chains ready to enter Taiwan and build hotels there. For such hotel construction the ban on large high-rise building starts has recently been lifted as an exception to the general rule. By the end of 1975 Taipei will have a new Holiday Inn with a planned 500 rooms. Other entrants and applications are being processed.

So much detail on travel and tourism might seem not too relevant to the main subject of this study, the new informal agencies for the conduct of relations between Japan and the Republic of China in the absence of formal diplomatic relations. But this emphasis is necessary if we are to understand the importance, implications and development of the case in Japan-ROC relations to which detailed consideration will be given in the balance of this study. This is the case of the Japan-Republic of China aviation agreement, to which reference has already been made. In the handling of this case in the relations between Japan and the ROC, the EARA and ICA played prominent parts. Just how did they operate, and how effective were they as exponents, advocates and representatives of the interests of their respective countries? There could hardly be a more important matter between Tokyo and Taipei than this one, a prime embodiment of their prosperous and profitable economic, social and cultural relations. It may be stated further, that the outcome of the negotiations between Peking and Tokyo and Tokyo and Taipei on this matter would materially affect the future conduct of Tokyo-Taipei relations through the two new informal organizations they had set up for the purpose. For example, both Japan and the ROC had adopted the practice of having their respective organizations, EARA and ICA, use their national-flag airlines as informal couriers of documents back and forth, such documents being bagged and then simply handed to airline flight personnel for safe delivery to organization personnel in the country of destination. Privacy of communications between home and overseas offices of these organizations was thus maximized as far as possible in the absence of regular diplomatic pouches handled by regular diplomatic couriers. This system for privacy of communications would be cut off completely in case the Japan Airlines and China Airlines (ROC) ceased to fly between the two countries. This is a practical example of the bearing of the airline agreement issue between the ROC and Japan upon their newly set up informal organizations for the conduct of affairs between them.

Discussions between the Japanese government and the Chinese Communists on the topic of airline connections between the mainland and Japan began almost immediately after the establishment of diplomatic relations between them in September, 1972. This subject was no doubt part of the subject matter of the summit talks between Chou En-lai and Japan's Premier Tanaka in Peking. The lower level talks that followed soon afterwards failed initially to achieve any results. This was because of the Chinese Communist demand that Japan must cancel Taipei's landing rights in Japan as a price of any agreement for air connections between Japan and the mainland.

As to this, Japan had good reason not to anticipate any such demand on the part of Peking. For, during most of the time since the Chinese Communist takeover on the mainland their ships had been calling at Japanese ports frequented routinely by ships flying the ROC flag. The simultaneous presence of ships of both Chinese regimes in Japanese ports had never drawn the slightest objection from the Chinese Communists. The same precedent existed as to Hongkong, where both ships and aircraft of the Peking and Taipei registry, and designated as the official flag-carriers of the ROC and the Chinese Communist regime, have for years frequented the same spatially tightly limited facilities, and often in fairly close proximity to each other. But now, a new element had been introduced into the picture, namely the demand by Peking, in this particular case and this case only, for exclusivity as to air navigation and landing rights in Japan. This can only be explained in terms of political warfare by Peking against Taipei, and of the same thing by Peking in respect to Japan itself. We shall see very soon just how the latter aspect of this political warfare campaign was designed by Peking to bear upon Japan. Its obvious bearing upon Taipei must be clearly visible and understandable and would seem to need little explanation. But what it meant as to the ROC will also soon become clear as we follow the often tortuous path of this development in Japan-ROC relationships.

Despite their initial shock over the Chinese Communist demand that they must cut off air communications with the ROC, by March 1973 the Japanese had a mission in Peking for the specific purpose of negotiating an air agreement. They persisted in trying to retain the Japan-ROC air linkage. But the Chinese Communists met this with a demand that any negotiations of an air agreement between them must be preceded by Japanese agreement on what they termed "basic principles," namely that of exclusivity of Peking's privileges, and the total exclusion of the ROC flag airline from Japan.

Japan's insistence upon trying to preserve the air link with Taiwan in fact produced a very strong statement in Peking by Liao Cheng-chih, the head in Peking of the "Sino-Japanese Friendship Association" in which he stated the Japanese negotiators "hadn't shown the proper spirit and he ventured to doubt Japanese sincerity." (AP dispatch from Tokyo in *China Post*, 16 March 1972.) He also referred to the proposal for a joint Japanese-Soviet development of Soviet oil resources in Siberia and the building of a pipeline to connect the oil fields with the port of Vladivostok on the Siberian east coast. He said that this would supply fuel for Soviet tanks and warplanes in the area and went on to state that Russia had 1,300,000 troops along its borders in the region and that the Russians were "a treacherous enemy, more imperialistic than the imperialists." His own country, he said, had bitter feelings about this proposal, and would have to take "counter measures" if it went forward. But to Japan the oil development project, important, even vital, as it was from an economic point of view, was tied to a politically vastly more important matter, namely the desire of Japan to recover from the USSR the four northern islands of Japan held by the Soviets since World War II. Premier Tanaka had lumped the two matters together in discussions with the Russians, obviously hoping to regain all or some of the islands under contention as a price for Japan's technical and financial assistance to the Russians in the oil matter. The territorial question of the islands had long since become a burning issue to all Japanese and is thus prime fodder for the political mills of all Japanese politicians. But the Soviets have steadily remained adamantly opposed to any return to Japan of the islands in question. This, it would seem, has helped motivate, and strongly, the Japanese tendency to seek accommodations of all kinds with Peking. But what the balance of profit is from their thus trying to play the balance of power game between the Russians and Chinese Communists, is another question.

The Japanese response to Peking's insistence upon first discussing the "basic principles" of exclusivity of air rights in respect to Japan was to state that they had no authorization to discuss anything beyond possible terms of an air agreement itself, and "that the Japanese delegation was not authorized to negotiate" on such "basic principles" that might involve what they termed "politics." (*China Post*, UPI despatch from Tokyo, 20 March 1974.) The Chinese Communists on their side, while insisting that China Airlines must be barred from Japan and that Japan must publicly acknowledge that its airline agreement with Taipei was "null and void," agreed as a practical matter to get on with the details of a Japan-Communist China air agreement. This, the Japanese negotiating team head in Peking said, showed that the Chinese in Peking "showed understanding of Japan's position in maintaining the existing air route between Taipei and Tokyo." But since the Chinese Communists would insist upon the condition that Taipei's flag-carrier be barred from Japan and that the existing ROC-Japan air agreement was "null and void," the Japanese must have been hoping that some other arrangement could be made for air traffic between Japan and Taiwan. This might involve non-flag-carrier operations by both Japan and the ROC, perhaps by some "private" airline on each side, thus avoiding the Chinese Communist sensitivity on the matter of Japan's treating the ROC, as they put it, as "another China," i.e., as being under the control of a recognized or recognizable government.

All these developments caused Mr. Mah Soo-lay, head of the ROC's EARA office in Tokyo, to give a warning on 19 March which in light of later developments, was highly prophetic. He stated in Tokyo during a meeting with pro-Nationalist Diet members of the ruling Liberal-Democratic Party of Japan that the air agreement then being negotiated on in Peking could "seriously affect Japan Air Lines (JAL) flight to Hongkong and beyond." (*Ibid.*) By this he clearly meant that if Japan and Peking entered into an air agreement on Communist China's terms of abrogation of the Tokyo-Taipei agreement and if China Airlines, the ROC's flag-carrier were to be barred from Japan, the obvious result would be that Japan Airlines would also be barred from Taiwan and therefore inevitably the Japanese civil air line would also be barred from Taiwan's air space zone.

That this would be a serious matter for Japan's flights from Tokyo to Hongkong and onward from there can be seen when we realize that Taiwan's air space zone is a rough rectangle between 21 degrees and 29 degrees North Latitude and 117.3 degrees and 124 degrees East Longitude. These are the dimensions of the Flight Information Region (FIR) and Air Defense Identification Zone (ADIZ). Civil aviation authorities monitor the former, and the military is in charge of the Air Defense Identification Zone as would be entirely natural and essential for national security. (*News from China,* 7 June 1973.)

If Japan's flights to Southeast Asia and beyond, which normally have transited Taiwan en route, were to be diverted outside the Taiwan FIR and ADIZ, there would be at least an added forty or fifty minutes of flight time to Hongkong and beyond. Such flights would have to enter the area of the Philippines before flying back in a northwesterly direction to Hongkong. This would not only be costly, but it would also tend to divert air passengers between Tokyo and Hongkong to other airlines enjoying direct routes and shorter flying times.

That such action would be taken by the ROC was clearly the content of Mr. Mah Soo-lay's warning in Tokyo in March. In June the *Central Daily News* of Taipei quoted an "authoritative source" in the ROC as saying: (*Ibid.*)

> "If Tokyo decides to alter the current Sino-Japanese Air Agreement in exchange for an air treaty with Peiping, the Republic of China will take extremely strong measures, including interception of Japanese commercial aircraft flying over the Taiwan area."

It also stated that:

> "In its eagerness to get Chinese Communist agreement for an air treaty, the Japanese government has been suggesting that CAL flights to Japan be shifted to some out-of-the-way airport."

This clearly, though "unofficially" confirmed the validity of Mr. Mah Soo-Lay's warning in Tokyo in March as having much more than his own personal opinion behind it.

Nevertheless (or perhaps even because of this), the Chinese Communists kept on insisting upon the exclusion of the ROC aircraft from major airports in Japan. (*China Post,* 21 June 1973, UPI dispatch from Tokyo, quoting *Mainichi Shimbun,* Tokyo.) The Japanese tried to resolve this problem by a proposal to the Chinese Communists that Peking's aircraft should fly into the new Narita airport under construction for Tokyo, while China Airlines should continue to use the old Tokyo Airport and the Osaka International Airport. But the Chinese at Peking rejected this idea. Red China was insisting that "it does not wish to see China Airlines (CAL) at Japanese airports where jetliners from Peking may make landings and departures." (*China Post* 22 June 1973, UPI dispatch from Tokyo.)

The attitude of the ROC government on all this was one of "no concessions." (*China Post,* 5 July 1973, quoting *United Daily News* of Taipei of previous date.) Thus we have the regime in Peking and the GROC both taking the same attitude on Japanese attempts to introduce compromises into the negotiations. This was perfectly logical in view of the fact that Peking was trying its best to injure Taipei and Taipei was resolved not to be injured at Peking's hands. Consequently the Foreign Ministry in Taipei finally issued a formal statement on 14 July which confirmed in every detail the *Central Daily News* report of the previous month, quoted above, stating that if Japan should yield to Chinese Communist demands, "disrupting the present Taipei-Tokyo air agreement," the Republic of China would retaliate and would "stop allowing any Japanese airplanes to land in or fly over the Republic of China." (*News from China,* 16 July 1973.)

On 15 July Mr. Osamu Itagaki, President of the Japanese Inter-Change Association in Tokyo, arrived in Taipei for a five-day visit to present the Japanese government's point of view on this matter. (*News from China,* 16 July 1973.) He stated that the Chinese Communists were bringing pressure upon Tokyo to scrap the Taipei-Tokyo air accord, but that "nothing definite has been done about this." He told his counterparts in Taipei that he had urged the Japanese government to preserve the status quo. While in Taiwan he inspected the offices of ICA there and consulted widely with various government and civic leaders in the ROC. No doubt at least partly for his benefit, during the time of his visit the Chinese press in Taipei discussed the issues on air travel between Japan and the ROC at some length, reiterating the very strong position that had already been taken by the Foreign Ministry in Taipei. It seems certain that Mr. Itagaki was told in plain and clear language that the ROC government would not find it possible to compromise at all as to the terms of the air agreement then in effect. He must have taken back an unequivocal statement to this effect to his home government.

Was it possible that the Japanese government could seriously consider jeopardizing its highly lucrative air traffic with Taiwan in order to secure an agreement with Peking that would not amount to more than one weekly flight between mainland China and Japan by each side, and which only a few persons would utilize? This was the estimate of traffic on a China mainland-Japan air route by Misami Terai, Director of the Aviation Bureau, Ministry of Transport, Tokyo, in a UPI despatch from Tokyo, published by *China Post,* Taipei, on 22 June 1973. Or did the Japanese government really believe that Taipei was bluffing with its "no compromise" stand and would not in turn jeopardize its own traffic Japan-Taiwan? Added to this, China Airlines used Tokyo as the departure point for all its increasingly profitable flights to the U. S. west coast, at first via Anchorage, and then via Hawaii. These flights by CAL were important not only monetarily, but also in terms of national pride and prestige. Was it these connections between the Republic of China and the United States that the Chinese Communists were really aiming at? Were they really desirous of entirely replacing with flights from mainland China to North America the air connections between the United States and the Republic of China? International air transportation has for much of its relatively short life thus far, been thought of in terms of national pride, prestige and other considerations of national interest, as much as, or more so, than in terms of dollars and cents economic advantage.

Whatever the specific interests at stake for Red China, Japan or the Republic of China, the latter of these held a clear view of the general issues involved for itself. This was clearly indicated to a group of seventy-one Japanese members of the Diet who visited in Taiwan in early October 1973, by the high authorities of the ROC government. At a meeting of these Diet members on 1 October with Premier Chiang Ching-kuo the Premier spoke broadly of the situation in East Asia and of the interests of the Republic of China and Japan therein. He reportedly told the Japanese Parliamentarians that under no circumstances would Taipei hold "peace" talks with Peking. (*News from China,* 1 Oct. 1973.) He stated to them his view that Japan's development of relations with the Mao regime would lead finally to Japan's accepting "Chinese Communist domination," and said that in his view Japan's recognition of Communist China ranked with the Mukden Incident of 1931, the Marco Polo Bridge Incident of 1937 and sneak attack on Pearl Harbor of December 1941 as one of Japan's "four major historical mistakes" during the 20th century. As a further embodiment of the "no compromise" attitude of the ROC with respect to the Chinese Communists he told the visiting Japanese guests that "It is the right of the Republic of China to recover the Chinese mainland and free the compatriots shut behind the Bamboo Curtain."

While none of this dealt directly with the big issue of air transport arrangements between the ROC and Japan, the inflexible "no compromise" attitude he evinced as to the Chinese Communists certainly must have helped put the air matters into a realistic framework of ROC attitudes for the visiting Japanese Parliamentarians.

At a reception he gave these visitors later the same day Vice President C. K. Yen of the Republic of China displayed an equally firm attitude on the Chinese Communists, "until final victory," while voicing his belief that the traditional friendship between the Chinese and Japanese people would not change.

At the same time, Mr. Hirokichi Nadao, head of the Dietmen's Council of Relations between the ROC and Japan, former Japanese Education Minister, and head of the Japanese delegation, denied a report in the *Asahi Shimbun* (Tokyo) that he had come to Taipei to persuade Taipei to accept the Japanese government's position on the air transport agreement it was working out with Peking. Two other Dietmen confirmed this, and it was stated that they had asked the *Asahi Shimbun* to publish a correction.

General Ho Ying-chin, President in Taiwan of the Sino-Japanese Cultural and Economic Association in an address to the visitors at a dinner in their honor, did warn Tokyo against doing anything that "would damage the Republic of China's civil aviation rights" in Japan. Such action, he warned, would have "serious consequences." The government in Taipei, he warned, was fully prepared to cope with any eventuality.

As a result of their visit to Taipei, the Dietmen's group on its return to Japan presented a request to Hogen Shinsaku, Vice Foreign Minister of Japan, that the terms of the existing air accord between Japan and the Republic of China not be changed. They pointed out that in their view, the reported Chinese Communist demand that the terms of the accord be changed constituted a case of interference in the internal affairs of Japan. They urged that before the terms of any Tokyo-Peking air accord were settled upon, the agreement should be submitted for the approval of the Liberal-Democratic Party. (*News from China,* 5 October 1973.)

In the meantime, Mr. Liao Cheng-chih in Peking continued to insist that it would be a "caricature" if airlines of the two rival regimes on Chinese soil both used the Tokyo Airport. And as a further inducement to the Japanese, an agreement had already been worked out with France for Japan Airlines and Air France jointly to operate a Tokyo-Peking-Paris route when the issue of Japanese flights into mainland China had been settled. (*South China Morning Post,* Hongkong, 20 October 1973.)

For their part the Overseas Chinese organizations in Japan put forward their views on the general question of Sino-Japanese relations and specifically on the air transport agreement problem in taking out a full-page advertisement in one of the Japanese newspapers on 12 November 1973. Some eighty of these Associations, headed up by the United General Association of Chinese in Japan, jointly sponsored this statement which surveyed the immediate background of Sino-Japanese relationships, the changes brought about by Japan's severing of relations with the ROC and entering into regular diplomatic relations with Peking, the various problems arising therefrom, etc. The main burden of their presentation focussed on the air transportation problem between Tokyo and Taipei and their strongly expressed position was one of support for Taipei and of opposition to any unilateral changes by Tokyo in the existing air agreement between Taipei and Tokyo. (*Sankei Shimbun,* Tokyo, 12 Nov. 1973.)

Although there were signs of incipient factional disagreements within the ruling Liberal Democratic Party in Japan over the question of what would happen to air communications between Japan and the Republic of China under the terms of the proposed air agreement with Communist China, this did not deter the Party leadership from proceeding to negotiate the matter with Peking. In early January 1974, Foreign Minister Ohira of Japan visited Peking for high-level talks. (New, N. S., "Why is Tanaka Letting Peiping Destry ROC-Japan Air Accord?", *Asian Outlook*, Feb. 1974, pp. 2-4.) He signed a trade agreement with Peking and on returning to Japan a six-point plan for an air agreement with the Chinese Communists was revealed. Under it, the Japanese proposed to preserve "the present air arrangements between Tokyo and Taipei," including rights to fly beyond these points, under a new accord "to be signed on the private level." Japan Airlines, the Japanese national flag carrier, would no longer fly to Taiwan, however, it being necessary to substitute some other "private" carrier for it. Japan would no longer use the name "China Airlines" but instead refer to "China Airlines (Taiwan)," and would otherwise also make its stand clear as to the flag of the Republic of China carried as identification insignia of China Airlines. Just how this was to be done was left unspecified, but this was later to become a critically important point in the whole matter. Use by the airlines of the ROC of airports separate and different from those to be used by Chinese Communist planes in Japan was to be arranged. And all independent China Airlines administrative operations in Japan were to be taken over from China Airlines by some other agency or enterprise, unspecified at that time.

But even before these proposals had emerged in Tokyo, the position of the Republic of China was again being stated in Taipei in the clearest possible terms and by the highest authorities there. On 15 January

Premier Chiang Ching-kuo had an interview with a visiting member of the Japanese Diet, Masayuki Fujio. (*News from China,* 16 Jan. 1974.) He told him that the ROC stood on the position it had enunciated the previous July against unilateral Japanese alteration of the ROC-Japan air route agreement. He warned against Japan's yielding to pressure from Communist China to make such changes, and repeated the determination of the ROC to make Japan responsible for any such disruption of the air route and to invoke prohibition of Japanese planes entering the Taiwan Air Defense Identification Zone if Japan were to "disrupt" the existing ROC-Japan air agreement. Prior to his departure from Taipei Mr. Fujio told the press there that he fully understood the firm stand of the ROC on this matter.

On the same day that Premier Chiang was issuing this renewed warning, Osamu Itagaki, President of Japan's Inter-Change Association, had stated in Taipei that there would not be any change in the Tokyo-Taipei flight arrangements. (*Ibid.*) He said, "I believe that the Republic of China will be able to carry through her purpose of maintaining the Taipei-Tokyo air route." He was present in Taipei at that time for a four-day visit. And Mr. Mah Soo-lay, Head of the ROC's East Asia Relations Association in Tokyo, returned to Taipei on January 24 for consultations with his people there, remaining until 20 February. (*News from China,* 27 Feb. 1974.)

On 9 February the ruling Liberal Democratic Party of Japan adopted a resolution to treat the Japanese aviation accords with Peking and Taipei as "parallel issues," and to conduct negotiations regarding them "simultaneously." (*Ibid.*) Some observers in Tokyo therefore reached the logical conclusion that the previously announced six-point plan for solving the problem had been set aside. This impression was supported by the statement made in Taipei on 26 February by Kiichi Arita, Japanese M. P. and former Education Minister, that Japan would "respect" its substantial relations with the ROC in negotiations for a new Taipei-Tokyo air transport accord. Arita, also Chairman of the Board of Trustees of the Japan-Republic of China Travel Association, was accompanied on his trip to Taipei by the President of his Association and a 28-member party. (*Ibid.*) The Association had been established in Japan on 15 February with fifty-four travel service companies as its members.

In accord with the LDP resolution of 9 February, on 28 February

Mr. Itagaki of the Japanese Inter-Change Association once again departed for Taipei, this time to negotiate a "non-governmental" civil aviation agreement between Japan and the ROC. Before leaving Tokyo he had called upon Mr. Mah, representative in Tokyo of the ROC's East Asia Relations Association, to formally notify the intent of his Association to open talks in Taipei for writing such a civil aviation agreement. On arrival in Taipei he was met at the airport by Chairman Chang Yen-tien of the East Asia Relations Association. (*News from China,* 28 Feb. 1974.) Negotiations proceeded.

On the day of Mr. Itagaki's arrival in Taipei the Executive Yuan of the Republic of China, in a written reply to a legislative interrogation, stated that the government would never accept any change in the current ROC-Japan air agreement that "may affect our national dignity and interests." (*News from China,* 1 March 1974.) This reflected the position of Premier Chiang Ching-kuo, affirmed in his administrative report at the opening session on 26 February of the Legislative Yuan, that Taipei would take "resolute and necessary action" if Tokyo should decide to "go it alone" on the issue of Taiwan-Japan air services. (*Ibid.*) And as the negotiations proceeded in Taipei with Mr. Itagaki, the ROC government through its East Asia Relations Association agreed to changes on two matters. (*China Post,* 5 March 1974.) These were (1) that Japan could substitute another Japanese air carrier other than Japan Airlines, the government-owned and operated airline, in the Japan-Taiwan service; and (2) that its own flag carrier, China Airlines, would agree to rearrange its schedules so that its planes would not be at any Japanese airport simultaneously with planes from Communist China. Other than these two changes, the ROC side refused any other and major changes in the air agreement.

On the Japanese side, Mr. Itagaki seemingly had nothing different to offer from those proposals made in January and based upon the six-point plan described above, and which had supposedly been shelved in favor of retaining as much as possible of the status quo. Critically unacceptable to the ROC in those previous six points were those involving the name of China Airlines, the ROC flag identification of China Airlines planes, and the handling of its business in Japan by its own representatives and staff members in accordance with normal practices of international air lines all over the world. The willingness of the Republic of China to make concessions on the two major points noted above did not seem to impress the Japanese negotiators in Taipei. One of them, who remained anonymous, stated in Taipei that "the Chinese position remains extremely firm," and that "there have been no developments, and there is really little room for discussion." (*Ibid.*)

In the meantime, the whole matter of the air pact with Taipei and the negotiations for a new one with Peking, had become, seemingly, an issue in the internal politics of the ruling Liberal-Democratic Party in Japan. ("Ohira and Sino-Japanese Air Pact," *The Japan Times,* 28 Mar. 1974.) Foreign Minister Ohira, as the focal point in the whole matter of the air agreements with Taipei and Peking, had come under attack, as much for the fact that the whole matter remained unsettled so long, as for the fact of resistance by pro-Taipei members of the Party to any sacrifice of the air relations between Tokyo and Taipei in the interest of getting a new agreement with Peking. The factional divisions in the Party were basically exploited, thus, by any and all Party members seeking to jockey for position in the sharing of Party power. Together with real declines in Party popularity in Japan due to the economic crisis of Japan, this further division of opinion in the Party was feared by Prime Minister Tanaka as a possible source of still further weakening of his political base in general. Therefore, along with Foreign Minister Ohira, he pushed for a quick solution of the whole tangled matter of the Sino-Japanese air agreements. The direction of their joint push was, however, entirely controlled by their joint and mutual commitment to total "normalization" of relations between Tokyo and Peking. Thus, any relatively "quick" solution of these matters would predictably take the form of sacrificing Tokyo's material interests in sustaining air connections with Taiwan in order to achieve an air transport agreement with Peking. This was the joint Tanaka-Ohira approach to the whole question.

The clear perception of this by the government of the Republic of China led to a series of signals to Tokyo, the meaning of which was crystal clear for the future of the air arrangements between Tokyo and Taipei. On 9 April the Control Yuan, characterized as "the nation's highest watch-dog body," adopted a resolution supporting the government's stand in the Tokyo-Taipei Civil Aviation issue. (*News from China,* 9 April 1974.) And the Legislative Yuan and the National Assembly also expressed their support for the government's stand. Two days later, 11 April, Foreign Minister Shen Chang-huan issued a formal statement on the subject. (*News from China,* 11 April 1974.) While rejecting as unacceptable the six-point proposal previously made by Tokyo, and denying that any real negotiations had been under way for a new "private" air arrangement between Tokyo and Taipei, the crux of Foreign Minister Shen's statement on the matter was as follows:

> "Should the Japanese Government, without our concurrence, unilaterally make changes to the existing Sino-Japanese civil aviation arrangement inimical to our national dignity and interests, the Government of the Republic of China shall take necessary measures in line with its policy as announced in its previous statements."

He went on to say that should the Japanese government take any such steps, "if need be, we shall not hesitate to give up the existing Sino-Japanese air route." He stated, as had been stated before, that this would mean that Japanese planes would no longer be permitted to land in the Republic of China or permitted to fly over the Taipei Flight Information Region or within its Air Defense Identification Zone.

As the Japanese trend toward unilateral action in respect to the Taipei-Tokyo air arrangements continued, and as absolutely no developments took place as to the negotiation between those two parties of any new air agreement, the government in the Republic of China put preparations under way for closing the Taipei-Tokyo air route. (*News from China*, 15 April 1974.) On 12 April, Chang Yen-tien, President of the East Asia Relations Association, had informed the Japanese Inter-Change Association office in Taipei of the stand contained in Foreign Minister Shen's statement of the previous day. He had also asked the Japanese organization to secure a prompt reply in writing to the points raised by the Shen statement, and to clarify the position of the Japanese government. This was occasioned by press reports in Tokyo based upon what was evidently a "leaked" report from the Tokyo Foreign Ministry made by a Japanese Diet Member, to the effect that Japan would soon declare that the Republic of China flag insignia of China Airlines was not considered "a national flag," and that China Airlines' counters in Tokyo International Airport would be closed down. (*Ibid.*)

After the relevant governmental (including military) authorities had met with aviation and informal organizational authorities of the East Asian Relations Association to prepare cessation of air communications of the Republic of China and Japan between the two countries, the local Taipei representatives of Japan Airlines were advised to prepare for the cessation of JAL activities in and with respect to Taiwan. At the same time, in order to be able to maintain its air link with the United States which had hitherto run through Tokyo, the government in Taipei exchanged views with the U. S. Embassy there as to an air traffic right of China Airlines to the United States through Guam instead.

These events took place on 14 April. The next day a number of governmental organs in Taipei backed up the stand of the administration there with supporting resolutions which were strongly worded. This included seven conveners of the Foreign Relations Committee of the National Assembly, not a legislative body but, in effect, the Electoral College of the Republic of China. As well, the Legislative Yuan on the same day adopted another resolution sponsored by 152 of its members, upholding the government's position. (*News from China,* 16 April 1974.) In both cases the statements emphasized the strong opposition of the parties concerned to action of a unilateral nature by the Japanese government, and which would "prove detrimental to our national interests and sovereignty."

Although it was rumored in Taipei that the air agreement between Tokyo and Peking would be signed on 20 April, this did not prevent a last-ditch attempt by the Japanese side to stall off the seemingly inevitable. On 17 April Mr. Itagaki, Chairman of the Japanese Inter-Change Association, arrived by air in Taipei to hold talks with the Chinese counterpart organization on the Tokyo-Taipei air route issue. (*News from China,* 18 April 1974.) Actual conversations between the representatives of the two organizations did not start until almost twenty-four hours after Mr. Itagaki's arrival in Taipei, when he had an opportunity to state the position of the Japanese government. The conversation lasted only thirty-five minutes, including time for translations. Mr. Itagaki, according to the Republic of China negotiators, did nothing but restate the previously unacceptable position of the Tanaka government as to the matter, and brought "no new proposals to Taipei." From this, the Chinese side stated, "It is clear that the Japanese Government has subserviently and irrevocably accepted the outrageous demands of the Chinese Communist regime." Nevertheless, the written statement of the Japanese position, which Mr. Itagaki had brought with him from Tokyo, was duly transmitted by Taiwan's Association of East Asian Relations to the government of the Republic of China. (*News from China,* 19 April 1974.) Mr. Chang Yen-tien, head of the East Asian Relations Association in Taipei was thereafter instructed to inform Mr. Itagaki, his opposite number of the Japanese organization, that the Republic of China government considered "the Japanese position as reflected in the written reply, to be seriously detrimental to the interests of the Republic of China."

On 20 April the Japanese government signed a civil air accord with the Chinese Communist regime and this was followed immediately by the closing of the Taipei-Tokyo air route by order of Foreign Minister Shen of the government of the ROC. (*News from China,* 20 April 1974.) This closure referred, of course, solely to airline operations of the two countries; all third-country airline operations between them went on without any interruption. It is vitally important here, as at all other points, to understand correctly the basis of this action by the Taipei authorities. Foreign Minister Shen's statement was clear as to the reasons behind the ROC's actions: (*Ibid.*)

> "But, anxious to conclude a civil aviation agreement with the Chinese Communist regime, the Tanaka Government totally disregarded the good-will of the Republic of China towards Japan. On the one hand, it subserviently submitted itself to Communist manipulations in accepting Peiping's unreasonable demands; and on the other, it ignored the firm and just stand of the Government of the Republic of China which has been made explicit to Japan on many occasions, thus jeopardizing the existing Sino-Japanese civil aviation arrangement. Moreover, Mr. Ohira, in his outrageous statement, cast reflection upon the national flag of the Republic of China, thereby impairing seriously the dignity and interests of the Republic of China, and inflicting serious damage once again upon the friendly relations between the Chinese and Japanese peoples, carefully fostered through their joint efforts since the end of the war."

It is clear from this statement that the government of the ROC evaluated the whole matter of air relations with Japan in the same way as did the regime of Mao Tse-tung, namely as part of Peking's political warfare to secure the total isolation of the government on Taiwan both diplomatically and substantively. Hence the emphasis of the ROC government upon the purely political considerations involved, namely the willingness of the government of Japan, under Chinese Communist pressure, to make an official and public statement casting "reflection upon the national flag of the Republic of China." The action of the

ROC in cutting off the air traffic agreement with Japan was thus clearly based upon a prime political consideration, namely the international upholding of its claim to political legitimacy as an independent sovereign state. The fact that Japan had already destroyed the normal previous diplomatic relations between Tokyo and Taipei by its establishment of such relations with Peking had not, up to then, resulted in serious disruption of substantive relations between Japan and Taiwan. What the Chinese Communists objected to was precisely the failure of a change in diplomatic relationships to impair materially the substantive relations between Japan and Taiwan. And by insisting upon the adoption by Japan of a formula as to the flag identification of China Airlines which did precisely state that such flag identification was to be publicly denied to have any political meaning in terms of any sovereign political entity, it chose the precise area of maximum political sensitivity in the ROC within which to exact its price for a Peking-Tokyo civil air accord. The reaction of the ROC to Japan's willingness to go along with Peking in this form of political warfare against Taipei was thus inevitable, as well as having been made entirely predictable by Taipei for months in advance of its being taken.

All this was clearly understood in Japan. In an article in *The Japan Times* of 21 April, the day after the action taken by the GROC, it was stated:

> "While the angry reactions of the Nationalist Government and of the pro-Taiwan elements in Japan were to be expected, they were directed not so much against the conclusion of the air accord [between Tokyo and Peking] as against the statement made by Foreign Minister Masayoshi Ohira on the status of Taiwan at the insistence of Peking."

On 23 April the same newspaper published a lengthy editorial on the matter, in which it was stated that Taiwan's cutting the air agreement between the two countries "did come as a shock to Japanese leaders, including Prime Minister Kakuei Tanaka and Foreign Minister Masayoshi Ohira, who had reckoned that Taiwan would not cut off this lucrative air link." It went on to say:

> "What has been revealed once more is the easy-going optimism of our leaders in their belief other nations have norms of value like their own. They should know that the pursuit of the GNP (gross

national product) and financial gain is not the only worthwhile endeavor in the eyes of other people. This is certainly true with Taiwan in this instance. . . .

And the direct cause of Taiwan's stern reaction was the statement made by Foreign Minister Ohira following the conclusion of the Sino-Japanese aviation accord. He made two points in particular—that the 'emblem' on the Nationalist aircraft would not be recognized as a 'national flag' and that the China Airlines operating from Taiwan would not be considered as representing a state.

Especially distasteful to Taiwan was the fact Japan was pressured into making this statement at the insistence of China. It was the Japanese 'price' for the aviation agreement, although it is clear that Peking had much more to gain than Tokyo from the new outlet."

The editorial went on to state that the cessation of its air traffic to and through Taiwan involved not only a financial loss and "the need for a lengthy detour in its air links with Southeast Asia," but a blow to Japan's dealings with Southeast Asian states which from then on would be convinced that Japan would be willing to sacrifice "a weaker neighbor" to the demands of the Chinese Communists. It went on to describe the general dilemma of Japan in future relations of a substantive nature with Taiwan:

"China, of course, realizes the existence of Taiwan as an independent entity. And that is why Peking is so insistent on seizing every opportunity to isolate Taipei from its neighbors. Caught between the reality of an independent Taiwan and the Chinese myth of a Taiwan under China, Japan can expect no lessening of its troubles in its future dealings with Peking."

Other Japanese opinion, however, was much more in line with the Tanaka-Ohira view of things and supportive of its actions in this case. For example, *Mainichi Shimbun* commented on the Ohira statement as follows: (Quoted in *The Japan Times,* 22 April 1974.)

"The statement is designed to clarify Japan's understanding of the name of Taiwan's airlines and the flag (the White Sun in the Blue Sky) of the aircraft. The Ohira statement was issued for the purpose of distinguishing China's airlines from Taiwan's. The terms of maintenance of the Tokyo-Taipei air route do not include drastic changes.

Moreover, it will no doubt contribute to stabilizing nongovernmental Tokyo-Taipei relations. We believe that the acceptance of the Tokyo-Peking aviation agreement will serve Taiwan best."

And the *Tokyo Shimbun* while expressing the hope that the whole matter would not have destructive political consequences within the Liberal-Democratic Party, stated that no one could predict how long the suspension of the Tokyo-Taipei air agreement would last, but that (Quoted in *ibid.*):

". . . there is little possibility that the latest development will trigger deterioration of trade and other relations with Taiwan. We sincerely hope that the Taipei Government which refrained from total severance of relations will exercise the same discretion hereafter in full cognizance of the wish of our people to keep our friendship with people in Taiwan as well as in China."

In the meantime, Osamu Itagaki, President of the Japanese Interchange Association, left Taipei and returned to Tokyo on 21 April. (*News from China,* 22 April 1974.) This had been his third visit to Taipei during 1974 for the purpose of working to preserve some sort of air traffic agreement that would allow both Japanese and ROC airlines to operate between the two countries. But all his efforts were fruitless. The final decisions in these matters were clearly not in his hands but in those of the Japanese Prime Minister and Minister of Foreign Affairs. Clearly both of these individuals considered the establishment of air traffic arrangements between Communist China and Japan so supremely important that they were willing to make political concessions to the Chinese Communists which would sacrifice their lucrative air traffic rights in respect to Taiwan. In the meantime, the ROC cancelled its air traffic to the Republic of Korea because its planes flying there from Taiwan had to fly within the Japanese Flight Information Region and Air Defense Identification Zone. The Japanese authorities decided not to bar planes from Taiwan from flying to Seoul through their air space, but the ROC authorities decided not to accept their offer. (*News from China,* 24 April 1974.) And as of 20 April all China Airlines traffic to the United States flew by way of Guam and Honolulu. (*Ibid.*, 22 April 1974.)

The Japanese Foreign Minister, in the meantime, made a statement in favor of the restoration of the air links Tokyo-Taipei. But the attitude of the ROC was clearly stated by the *United Daily News* of Taipei: "Japanese talk of a reopening is meaningless. The harm has been done.... Even after Japan recognized Peiping the two peoples maintained harmonious relations. But the Ohira statement which said the Republic of China's flag does not represent a sovereign nation is an insult to the Chinese government and people." (*Ibid.*) And the English-language *China News* of Taipei stated: (*Ibid.*, 23 April 1974.)

> "There is a solution. There has been one all along.
>
> The Peiping-Tokyo air agreement is not to our liking but we have never said we would try to interfere with flights between Japan and the mainland.
>
> The government even agreed to accept a JAL subsidiary for Tokyo-Taipei flights. What the Japanese wish to call their airlines is their own business.
>
> We want from Japan only what we offer Japan. We want to fly there and beyond, as we have for many years, under any name we wish and in airliners bearing insignia of our own choice. We want our own ground personnel to handle these flights. This, too, is reciprocal.
>
> That's all. This is not asking for anything. It is maintenance of the status quo. If the Japanese cannot do this without losing their right to fly to the Chinese mainland, then Japan has already passed into a condition of international servitude."

In the meantime, the seven other airlines flying between Japan and Taiwan were enjoying a boom in their traffic, to take up the slack caused by the cancellation of the some thirty JAL and some twenty CAL flights each week between the two countries. All were planning to add extra flights to their existing schedules, or at least to use larger planes than had previously been in use. (*Ibid.*) But by May the Japanese government had turned down requests by other airlines to increase the number of their flights Japan-Taiwan. (*Ibid.*, 3 May 1974.) This was no doubt in order to maximize pressures on the ROC to come to some sort of new agreement for air rights. But on the other hand, the pressures on Japan itself were not slight. The *Japan Times* of Tokyo reported that annual earnings from the now suspended Taiwan-Japan air traffic by JAL totalled US$49 million, or about ten percent of its total earnings worldwide. (*Ibid.*, 23 April 1974.) The annual profit from JAL's operations to and from Taiwan was estimated at US$29 million.

And this left out of account the extra cost to JAL of its new and longer route to Hongkong and Southeast Asia from Japan, which had to run via Okinawa and the northern Philippines in order to avoid entry into Taiwan's air space. This route was estimated to be 559 miles farther with an estimated extra flight time of fifty minutes. All this affected the JAL traffic to and from Hongkong and points further within Southeast Asia.

Political consequences in Japan would logically be expected to arise over all this. On 24 April there was a report from Taipei that four vice ministers of the Tanaka administration and two ranking officials of the ruling Liberal-Democratic Party in Japan had resigned over the issue. (*Ibid.*, 24 April 1974.) Although this was later denied in Tokyo, and *The Christian Science Monitor* stated in its issue of 26 April that "The break in Japan-Taiwan air relations has quickly fizzled out as a political issue in Japan," the *Mainichi Daily News* of 11 May stated that:

> "Nothing in recent months shook Prime Minister Tanaka's prestige, particularly concerning his leadership of the party, so badly as the intra-party ruckus that flared up in the course of gaining one air pact and losing another."

And this was generally confirmed by the *Economist* (London) which reported in a despatch from Tokyo in late April that however much the economic loss involved would concern Japan Airlines, it would matter even more to Prime Minister Tanaka who had convinced himself and others that Japan could have it both ways with Peking and Taipei, and that as a result he and his Foreign Minister were being attacked by the right wing of their party for betrayal of the interests of the Republic of China.

Predictably (cf. *The Christian Science Monitor* for 26 April 1974) a move was being discussed under which the intra-party fight over the air pacts Tokyo-Peking and Tokyo-Taipei would be compromised without sacrifice to Prime Minister Tanaka but to cost the Foreign Minister, Mr. Masayoshi Ohira, his cabinet post. This was to come after the upper house election in the Japanese Diet in July.

In the meantime, in a speech before the Commonwealth Club of San Francisco on 27 April, Dr. Frederick F. Chien, Director-General of the Government Information Office of the GROC, told his audience that his government's decision to terminate any air agreement with Tokyo was not made simply because Japan had signed such an accord with the

Chinese Communists, but mainly because of Japanese Foreign Minister Ohira's having made a "very, very insulting" statement at the time of signing, to the effect that Japan did not recognize the Republic of China as a sovereign nation. (*News from China,* 27 April 1974.) What he was saying in effect was that the absence of formal diplomatic relations between Japan and the ROC could not excuse a flagrant insult to the ROC's national flag and its designation by the Japanese Foreign Minister as a mere "trademark." Would, for example, the fact that the ROC had no diplomatic relations with Japan be a justification for some such remark by the ROC Foreign Minister about the national flag of Japan? That the Japanese Foreign Minister's remark was part of a price insisted upon by the Chinese Communists for their agreeing to a bilateral air agreement between Peking and Tokyo only made what the Japanese Foreign Minister said all the more unendurable to Taipei and all the more gratuitously insulting from Taipei's point of view. It is hard to credit the Japanese Foreign Minister with much less than a most formidable lack of any sort of diplomatic finesse in the case in question. If he had been most deliberately trying to injure the structure of *de facto* relations cultivated between Japan and the ROC since the rupture of diplomatic relations between them previously, he could not have succeeded better than he in fact did by his action in this connection.

What of these *de facto* relations, then? How were they faring? The first area of damage has been seen in the effect upon the annual profit balances of Japan Airlines. But the ROC's interests were of course not immune. During the nine-day period following the cancellation of JAL and CAL flights, the number of Japanese tourists coming into Taiwan fell to 940 a day compared with the daily average of 1,929 for the first three months of 1974, representing a drop of 49%. (*News from China,* 1 May 1974.) This was due no doubt to inevitable disruption of travel plans and the need for the Japanese tourists who had almost all travelled by their national airline, to transfer to other airlines. Most of them had been booked on relatively inexpensive group travel plans with JAL. But by the end of April the first effects of flight cancellations had begun to taper off, and the number of Japanese tourists had begun to rise again. And by October it was possible to calculate the whole tourist influx for the first half of the year, and to discover that despite the falloff of Japanese tourists entering Taiwan, the tourist picture as a whole was excellent for Taiwan.

Total numbers of tourists entering Taiwan during the first nine months of 1974 had actually increased, it was found, by a total of 6.9% over the corresponding period of 1973. (*News from China,* 18 October 1974.) Japanese tourists numbered 349,242 or a daily average entering the ROC of 1,281, as compared to a daily average of 1,929 entering during the first three months of 1974. But this loss of about 700 Japanese tourists daily was more than made up for by increases from other places, to bring the total to the 6.9% over the previous year's number. This was at a time when generally speaking tourism in other important world centers was falling off.

China Airlines suffered a revenue loss estimated at US$23 million from the stoppage of its flights to Japan and return. (*News from China,* 10 May 1974.) The combination of JAL and CAL flight cancellations has generally speaking left available, at total booking of seats in other airlines, only some 60% of the capacity needed for the traffic between Japan and Taiwan. The ROC stood willing to allow increased flights between Taiwan and Japan by third-country lines but the Japanese government refused to allow this. Here it must be remembered again that the two-way trade between Taiwan and Japan has always been heavily balanced in favor of Japan, and that the large Japanese tourist flow into Taiwan helps to keep the total picture from being entirely too unfavorable to Taiwan.

At first, the CAL flights to the United States, re-routed by way of Guam for refuelling, were mostly very lightly loaded. But this soon changed, and the flights by May were fully loaded, mostly with American businessmen. And CAL quickly initiated an augmented air freight service between Taiwan and the United States and other points. By June 1 an all-cargo service was begun between Kaohsiung and Taipei in Taiwan and Los Angeles and San Francisco. As well, a direct cargo service was begun between Taipei and Hongkong and Singapore.

In Southeast Asia, the Malaysian government established diplomatic ties with Communist China, but to the contrary of what had happened in the case of Japan, the air services between Malaysia and Taiwan were not suspended. (*News from China,* 3 May 1974.) The ROC government terminated its consular services in Malaysia after that government took up diplomatic relations with Peking. However, the Malaysian Airlines and China Airlines offices began to serve as the main channels for obtaining visas for travellers. (*New York Times,* 16 June 1974.) And both Jordan and Saudi Arabia began to negotiate for landing rights in Taiwan en route, they hoped to Japan, thus augmenting passenger capacity between the two countries. Since the ROC is on excellent terms with both, and Japan, with considerations of oil supply in mind, would be likely to approve, this was a favorable prospect for the future of travel between the two countries.

The clearly political nature of the situation regarding relations with China in Japan was indicated in June when an attempt was made to oust the Tokyo Bureau Chief, Lee Chia, of the ROC's Central News Agency of China from membership in the Foreign Correspondents Club (FCC) of Tokyo. (*News from China,* 6 June 1974.) Lee, a life member of FCC and former President, was then serving as Treasurer and Board Director of the Club. The Chinese Communists persistently demanded the ouster of Mr. Lee from the FCC as a condition of their own entry, and Gregory Clark, an Australian correspondent in Tokyo acted for them in the general membership meeting where he moved to call a special committee into being to gain admission for the Chinese Communists within two months. He specifically claimed that with the imminent opening of direct flights between Tokyo and Peking, the admission of Chinese Communist reporters into the FCC had become "an urgent matter."

Mr. Lee Chia, the Agency Head from Taipei, for his part, welcomed any qualified journalist to the Club, irrespective of his ideology, showing in this case another clear contrast between the Chinese Communist demand for exclusivity of rights and the ROC's willingness to accept a condition of mutuality of rights. The Club membership voted overwhelmingly against any possible compromise with the Chinese Communists on their demand for exclusivity of membership or on any proposal to make Mr. Lee Chia some sort of inferior member with no right to vote, in order to gain entry of the Chinese Communists. Members from the other Communist bloc nations voted against the proposal. One of them said he had walked into the Club himself to fill out an application for membership, and asked why the journalists from Communist China could not do the same thing.

By mid-June, some two months after the rupture of air transport arrangements of the Japanese and ROC airlines running between Taiwan and Japan, it had become apparent that although considerable difficulties had been anticipated, "the difficulties encountered so far appear to be minimal." (*New York Times,* 16 June 1974.) This was in spite of the refusal of the Japanese government to allow third country airlines to increase their flights between Japan and Taiwan to take up the slack created by suspension of flights by CAL and JAL. In fact, it was expected in Taipei that after the Upper House elections in Japan in July, the Japanese government might approach Taipei for some arrangement by which flights by the two airlines in question might be renewed, or at least some arrangement made by which aircraft of the two countries, whether or not they were flag-carriers of the governments involved, could renew the traffic.

The attitude of the government in Taipei on this was clear. "What we objected to was not the signing of an air agreement between Japan and Peking, but the statement by Mr. Ohira that was detrimental to our interests and dignity," said one senior Foreign Ministry official in Taipei. (*Ibid.*)

On 17 June there was in fact an appeal by Parliamentary Vice-Ministers to the government in Tokyo to step up efforts for the resumption of air services of the two countries between Japan and Taiwan. (*China Post*, 19 July 1974.) On the same date, no doubt as a consquence, the ROC Foreign Minister Shen Chang-huan, testifying before a closed-door meeting of the Foreign Affairs Committee of the Legislative Yuan, stated again that the reason his government had severed the Tokyo-Taipei air link on 20 April was that the Japanese government had taken action detrimental to the "interest and dignity of the Republic of China." He went on to say: "Unless these factors are remedied, the Republic of China will not take any consideration to resume the air service." (*News from China*, 18 June 1974.) The next day Mr. Mao Yin-tsu, Director of the Civil Aeronautics Administration of the ROC, stated that the Japanese knuckling down under Chinese Communist pressure and the Tanaka government's "insulting remarks" about the ROC had been the principal cause of the disruption of the air link Japan-Taiwan. (*Ibid.*, 19 June 1974.) And the Hon. Hsieh Jen-chao, a Convenor of the Foreign Affairs Committee of the Legislative Yuan, said that if Japan could make amends for its previous actions, chances of restoring the air services "are good." He further stated: "Once the cause that led to the disruption of the air link between Free China and Japan is removed, I see no reason why we should object to the resumption of air service between the two countries."

But press opinion in Taipei was more pessimistic. On 19 July the

Chung Hua Jih Pao of Taipei stated its opinion that there was no possibility of reopening the Japan-Taiwan air services of CAL and JAL. (Quoted in *Free China Weekly,* 28 July 1974.) By then the resignation of Foreign Minister Ohira from the Tanaka Cabinet had taken place, and Toshio Kimura had taken his place. About him the *Chung Hua Jih Pao* said:

> "We don't believe the new Japanese foreign minister Toshio Kimura, will change the Tanaka government's policy toward the Republic of China.
>
> Kimura is pro-Maoist and will continue the efforts of his predecessor, Masayoshi Ohira, to please the Chinese Communists.
>
> The new foreign minister said he hoped to conclude a 'peace treaty' with the Chinese Communists and reopen civil aviation relations with the Republic of China. The two goals are incompatible."

A somewhat more moderate view, however, was expressed about the same time by the *United Daily News* of Taipei (*Lien Ho Pao*). Quoted in English translation by *China Post* of Taipei on 22 July, *United Daily News* stated in effect that the whole issue was that of Foreign Minister Ohira's statement of 20 April 1974, and that the basic premise upon which any renewal of air traffic by the two countries between Japan and Taiwan rested had to be the revocation by Premier Tanaka of Japan of the Ohira statement of that date. This statement deserves to be quoted fully as to its relevant part:

> "The statement referred the Red China-Japanese civil air agreement was [sic] a 'nation-to-nation' one, while the ROC-Japanese agreement was a 'regional and non-governmental one.'
>
> It also said that the Japanese government will not consider the flag the CAL planes carry as representing the national flag of the ROC, nor does it consider the CAL as a company representing the ROC.
>
> Such humiliating expressions can hardly be tolerated by both the government and the people of the Republic of China.
>
> In a word, if Kimura's answer to this basic premise is in the affirmative, we may consider talking about the resumption of Sino-Japanese civil aviation, otherwise everything is meaningless."

On 29 July Foreign Minister Shen stated again before the 1974 National

Reconstruction Seminar in Taipei that it was former Foreign Minister Ohira's remarks upon signing the air accord with Peking on 20 April that had prompted the ROC to terminate the then existing air accord with Tokyo. (*News from China,* 29 July 1974.) He said those remarks had seriously damaged "the dignity and sovereignty of the Republic of China." This was his first statement after the new Foreign Minister of Japan, Toshio Kimura, had stated his hope to restore the Taipei-Tokyo air service by China Airlines and Japan Airlines as soon as possible. (*Free China Weekly,* 4 August 1974.) In fact, the *Tokyo Shimbun* had reported that Foreign Minister Kimura had approached Mr. Shiina, Deputy Director of the Liberal Democratic Party, urging him to support the resumption of the air route arrangements between Japan and Taiwan. (English-language translation from *China Times,* Taipei in *China Post,* 27 July 1974.) The *China Times* commented as follows:

> "As we have pointed out before, our government has been holding a tolerant attitude towards Japan. Negotiations between our two countries about anything will not be impossible if our national dignity is not damaged and if our established principle is not violated. The resumption of the air route should be no exception."

This was followed by the announcement in Tokyo on 30 July that Mr. Naka Funada, former speaker of the Japanese House of Representatives and a senior member of the ruling Liberal Democratic Party of Japan would visit Taipei with another LPD member to attend the Third Sino-Japanese Symposium on Communist Affairs 9-10 September, as observers. (*News from China,* 1 Aug. 1974.) It was speculated by some political observers in Taipei that this might lead to some sort of breakthrough on the air transport question. Mr. Funada was expected, during his stay in Taipei, to consult with persons previously or at that time influential in ROC-Japan relations.

However, although Prime Minister Tanaka told Mr. Funada before his Taipei visit that he hoped for "closer cultural, economic and personnel interchanges with the Republic of China," Mr. Funada himself said he would not bring up for discussion in Taipei the resumption of the air service between Tokyo and Taipei. (UPI Despatch from Tokyo, in *China Post,* 7 Sept. 1974.)

It is quite probable that the determining factor in the stalemate that seems to have developed between the Republic of China and Japan as to possible renewal of their commercial flights between the two countries emerged from a different but related set of factors in the developing relations between Japan and Communist China.

This was the initiation during 1974 of talks between Tokyo and Peking on the matter of an agreement on shipping between Japan and the Chinese mainland. These talks had gone on for months before they were suspended without any agreement being reached, and the delegation from Peking left Tokyo and returned home. (UPI despatch from Tokyo, in *China Post,* 3 August 1974.) No reason was given out for the suspension of the talks, but the *Yomiuri Shimbun* of Tokyo stated that the basic cause had been the demand by Communist China for exclusivity of rights for its shipping in Japanese ports, the Chinese Communist requirement being that ships carrying the flag of the ROC had to be barred from Japanese ports if any shipping agreement was to be reached between Tokyo and Peking.

Whatever its attitude had been on exclusivity as applied to air traffic rights, the Japanese government was practically compelled to reject the Chinese Communist demand for such exclusivity as applied to shipping in Japanese ports. Japan Air Line's profits from its air traffic between Japan and Taiwan were hardly a mere bagatelle. But if shipping arrangements between Japan and Taiwan were to be totally disrupted by Peking's demand for, and ROC refusal to agree to, a Chinese Communist exclusivity in ocean shipping rights in Japanese ports, this would cause a very heavy blow at the Japanese economy. For the total trade between Japan and Taiwan, which had amounted to about US$1 billion a year in 1970-71, with a favorable balance to Japan of over US$500 million, had by 1974 very greatly increased. In the first nine months of 1974 the trade Japan-Taiwan had a favorable balance to Japan of over US$1.052 billion. (*China Post,* 15 October 1974.) And although air passengers and freight could be carried by third-country airlines, there could be no possible substitute for ROC and Japanese shipping in the carriage of almost all items entering into the foreign trade of the two countries with each other.

There could be no doubt but that it would be almost inconceivable, therefore, for Japanese negotiators of a Peking-Tokyo shipping accord to finally, in this matter, agree entirely to the consistent Chinese Communist demand for exclusivity of rights vis-à-vis shipping from the ROC in Japanese ports. But, no doubt related to this, the Japanese, having reached impasse with the Chinese Communists in this respect, would be most reluctant to "rock the boat" in their relations with Peking by trying to get, by whatever compromise possible, a renewal of some sort of air transport agreement between Tokyo and Taipei. It is therefore not too surprising that since early August, 1974, there has seemingly been absolutely no movement at all on either side toward the possible renewal of the Tokyo-Taipei air links. The matter has simply fallen into a complete impasse, seemingly, and from what evidence is publicly available. Both sides are evidently "sitting tight" on the present status where air traffic between them is entirely carried by third-country airlines.

As stated above, these other airlines would like to expand their services in order to be able to accommodate all the passengers previously flying between Japan and Taiwan, but have been prevented from doing so by the Japanese government's unwillingness to give them permission to expand their schedules.

The result is that in spite of their use of large-capacity aircraft, there has developed a rather tight bottleneck in the Tokyo-Taipei segment of international commercial aviation, particularly as involving passenger traffic. To illustrate the effect we can take the case of USA passengers bound for Taipei. There is only one US airline which carries passengers without change of airline, through Tokyo from the USA to Taiwan. This airline's flights from Japan to Taiwan, like those of other airlines, are almost monopolized, and are filled to capacity, by the still heavy Japanese tourist business to Taiwan. As a result, therefore, while a would-be air passenger between New York and Taipei can quite easily get to Tokyo from New York, he finds on seeking onward passage to Taipei that all seats are taken for months in advance. This applies equally to all airlines in the Japan-Taiwan business. The result, peculiarly enough, is that the only way to a quick and dependable booking from the USA to Taipei is to book a US domestic airline to the west coast, and then take China Airlines flights running daily from either San Francisco or Los Angeles across the Pacific to Taipei via Honolulu and Guam. Thus, indeed, is China Airlines making up in US dollars what it has lost in Japanese Yen. This is indeed an unexpected twist of fate, namely that through the obduracy of the Japanese government in refusing to agree to the augmentation of air schedules between Japan and Taiwan by third-country flag carriers, it contributes steadily to an increasing hardening of the attitude in Taipei toward negotiating further with it as to a renewal of Tokyo-Taipei civil air arrangements. This is hardly a favorable augury for any future real and material adjustment between the two countries on this matter. In the meantime, China Airlines is ordering wide-bodied jets from the United States to augment the capacity of its own flights.

But it is not too much to expect that by now the Japanese may have learned something from this affair. What must they have learned? Specifically, that once you start giving up something in your relations with the Chinese Communists, you will be forced by them, to the limit of their ability, to give up more, and still more. Indeed, if you but give the Chinese Communists a small paring of your fingernail, they will try to take your arm off all the way up to the shoulder, preferably, from their point of view, hacking it off with a blunt instrument. Thus, exclusivity, so lightheartedly conceded to the Mao regime by Japan in air transport arrangements where it involved a sacrifice of some thirty millions of U. S. dollars a year in profits, was thereupon extended in principle by the Chinese Communists to an area of Tokyo-Taipei economic relations, that of shipping, where the stake became one of some US$1.052 billions a year in favorable balance of trade to Japan.

It can easily be predicted, therefore, that the Japanese who negotiate matters of a substantive nature with Peking will have to learn that costs exacted by Peking are always cumulative in nature, and that they multiply in a rapid ratio to profits to those with whom the Chinese Communists negotiate.

Does this mean that the Chinese Communists do not count their own profits in economic terms and that, therefore, they are quite willing to demand terms from Japan regarding shipping that will preclude stabilization of shipping arrangements between the two countries that they themselves would profit from? The answer is in the affirmative, not because the Maoists are immune to the motive of economic profit, but because they always put politics first, in everything. In the case of Japan, this means that all economic policy is directed toward the Chinese Communist aim of eventually isolating and destroying the Republic of China and everything it stands for. They can have no security themselves, even in their own territory, until that objective is achieved. For to them, and in very reality, the ROC represents everything in the modernizing Chinese revolution of our time the total destruction of which is a *sine qua non* of the completeness of their own revolution. And they know full well that to millions of their own subjects on the Chinese mainland the Republic of China is an ever-present alternative to their own regime. As such, it goes on from one success to another in its own development, economic, social and cultural, a fact that no Chinese anywhere can be blind to.

In the face of the demands of the Chinese Communists for exclusivity in their substantive relations with Japan, the Republic of China is increasingly turning away from Japan and toward other alternatives. Its current "buy American" campaign is specifically designed to lessen its economic interdependence with Japan, with the eventual aim of reducing Japan's profits from the Taiwan trade at a time when any great profits from trying to increase Japan's trade with the Chinese Communists are a very poor prospect. And other countries having relations with Communist China, such as Canada, are steadily increasing their economic relations with Taiwan, and by no means providing the Chinese Communists with any support for their exclusivity motif.

No one can doubt but that the present instabilities in the political picture in Japan are related to an assessment by Japanese politicians and the public, of where the economic policies of their leaders have been bringing them. It must be clearly understood, however, that this type of thing is clearly within the Chinese Communist "game plan" for Japan which is dependent for its ultimate objective, namely the complete political takeover of Japan, precisely upon the disruption of Japanese politics and the breaking of the hold upon it which has been continuous for the past decades of the chief "big interests" in Japan. They cannot and will not always gain continuously in this game, but they work at it with assiduous long-term application. The recent prediction by a high Japanese economic authority (*New York Times,* 17 Oct. 1974) that Japan faces a major depression in 1975, cannot but deepen the dilemma of Japan in trying to deal with the Chinese Communists. For, the same expert says, there is hope that such a depression might be avoided provided highly inflationary wage settlements with the Japanese unions can be avoided next spring. Can anyone doubt that the leaders of these unions, very leftist or even communist in their orientations and affiliations, know precisely what they are and have been doing by their successive highly inflationary wage demands year after year? In the present critical state of the world economy and with

Japan pressed to the wall by rising costs of all kinds, it is predictable that the Chinese Communist influence will be brought to bear upon all leftists in Japan to accentuate, and not to relieve, the economic crisis of that nation. Thus, the Chinese Communist game plan for the destruction of the Liberal Democratic Party's leadership of Japan and the takeover of parliamentary and governmental power in Japan by a coalition of leftist parties and cliques will be strongly forwarded, and, who knows, may even come to complete fruition within the clearly foreseeable future. The ultimate objective of it is clearly to create a general exclusivity of Chinese Communist influence and power in Japan, evict the influence of the west including in particular that of the United States, and thus, as said above, create a new "Greater East Asia Co-prosperity Sphere," this time under Chinese Communist control. Within such a framework the Maoists would assume that the future of Taiwan would become a mere pawn in the much larger game of power politics in the western Pacific.

In the meantime, the Japanese government seems to have retained its belief in the value of the informal arrangements between it and the GROC for the conduct of the relations between the two countries and their people. It was reported on 24 October 1974 that Hironori Ito, incumbent Director of the Taipei office of the Japanese Inter-Change Association, and former Minister in the Japanese Embassy in Taipei, would be replaced in Taipei by Oshio Urabe, former Japanese Ambassador to the Philippines. (*News from China,* 24 Oct. 1974.) Mr. Ito would be recalled to a position in the Foreign Ministry in Tokyo.

It was also reported that Teizo Horikoshi, President of the Inter-Change Association in Japan, and Sadao Iguchi, a Director of the Association, would come to Taipei on 27 October to join in the celebration of the birthday of President Chiang Kai-shek on October 31. While in Taiwan they would call on governmental leaders and inspect the operations of the Inter-Change Association offices there. They did arrive on 27 October as scheduled (*News from China,* 28 Oct. 1974) and the next day they were followed by a 130-man mission from the Japanese Diet, including 70 members of ten factions of the ruling Liberal Democratic Party, six former Diet members, their aides, staff, etc. (*Ibid.,* 29 Oct. 1974), all on a single chartered aircraft of Cathay Pacific Airlines. This was planned in order to allow the Japanese Parliamentary group to "extend felicitations to President Chiang Kai-shek on his birthday," which was on 31 October.

While in Taipei the Japanese Diet members had numerous contacts with the very high-level members of the ROC officialdom. But, as Mr. Hirokichi Nadao, former Education Minister in the DLP Cabinet and a Lower House Member of the Diet explained, these contacts were such as hardly to allow for any sort of systematic discussion of problems and issues such as the possible renewal of airline contact between the two countries, which, he said, was not discussed. He stated the current position of his government as being in favor of such renewal, but as unable to come up with a formula under which this could be done. Clearly, the Tanaka Cabinet was intent upon allowing a still further period of development of airline ties between Japan and mainland China before again trying to go about arranging for a settlement of the knotty problem of renewal of an air agreement between Japan and the Republic of China.

By elevating the rank of their office chief in Taipei and by their protocol in respect to the birthday of the Chief Executive of the ROC, the Japanese seemed to be expressing their renewed faith in the informal organization for the conduct of relations between Tokyo and Taipei. Up to this date, what should be our verdict on the Sino-Japanese private organizations for the conduct of relations between the two countries?

In this study detailed analysis of the operation of this system for the international conduct of relations between two nations that do not have formal diplomatic relations has focussed strongly on one case, namely that of the air transport arrangements between them. We have seen that nothing either the Japanese or ROC organization could do could, seemingly, prevent a complete break in the air transportation arrangements between them, specifically as to the operations of their own flag-carrier air lines between Japan and Taiwan and thence to other points.

The real question, however, is not whether the efforts on both sides to prevent the rupture of their air transport relationship did or did not succeed. The real question must be rather as to how well and effectively the two organizations operated in this situation as the mutually contacting agencies of the two countries, and charged with the responsibility of informing each other and negotiating with each other.

Here, it seems clear that on both sides, the two informal organizations did function well. There cannot be discovered any real lapse in their primary job of keeping each other informed, and thus of keeping the governments on both sides informed, as to the positions of the two governments, as these positions on the matter in hand developed through time and by reason of the flow of events. Nor was there, as far as can be discovered, any real delay in the flow of information merely because of the interposition between the two governments of another organization in each country which is not a part of its "normal" diplomatic establishment for the conduct of international relations. The operatives of the two organizations, mainly professionals in "normal" diplomacy, functioned swiftly. They were in constant touch with their home offices and through them with the government departments involved in the matter in hand. The failure to maintain the air transport agreement between their two countries did not come about through any hampering or hindering effect which the two new organizations had on the functioning bureaucracies of their two countires.

Nor is there any indication of a hampering, hindering or delaying of the negotiations between the two countries on account of the need for such negotiations to be conducted directly between representatives of the two informal organizations instead of between accredited members of the diplomatic corps thereof. On the contrary, with a swift and regular flow of information to the governmental policymakers from and through the two informal organizations, their respective policymakers were quite openly and plainly in full charge of affairs. They simply delegated to their respective agents in the new organizations the regular carrying of such information and messages to the other side, again through the new organizations, as would have been done by members of the established diplomatic establishments of their respective countries if they had, in fact, been having regular diplomatic relations with each other.

Equally clearly, the top policymakers in both Japan and the Republic of China did, on occasion, make their own public announcements designed to reach the other side through the press and other media of communication, just as is so commonly done under circumstances of normal diplomacy. But there is no indication that they felt inclined to do any more or any less of this than would have been done if they had been in a state of normal diplomatic relations with each other.

It may perhaps be considered too early, at this time, to reach any firm conclusion as to whether, in a condition of having no regular diplomatic relations with each other, two countries can, in fact, preserve substantially the whole measure of their real and substantial relations with each other in such areas as business and commerce, cultural exchange, travel and transportation and financial dealings. This problem in the case in hand is greatly complicated by the fact that the rupture of diplomatic relations between Japan and the Republic of China involved a shift in Japanese diplomatic relations from one government claiming to be the rightful representative of "China," to another such regime with the same claim. The two Chinese claimants are, and have been, at war with each other for a very long time, with no end in sight to this condition of belligerency. That their warfare fluctuates greatly as to the degree of its conduct through use of arms by both sides, and that today it is largely a warfare in the realms of politics and economics, does not make it any the less intense or of any less deadly intent on both sides. This war, like many others in the past, must involve third parties, and especially so if such third parties have important relations with both combatants. Hence, in the case of Japan, that country and its government and people have found it impossible to escape fully the cost of being caught in situations of involvement with both Peking and Taipei.

In the matter of the Tokyo-Taipei air transportation arrangements the Japanese government sacrificed these arrangements in favor of such arrangements Peking-Tokyo. The costs here were borne by Tokyo and Taipei, and Peking reaped all the gain, whether economic (slight, only, for the foreseeable future), or political, where the gains at Taipei's expense were large. Depending upon the future course of Tokyo-Peking relations, Japan might have gained very materially in the political field by this concession of a highly profitable (economically) air traffic Japan-Taiwan. But the undoubted heavy loser in both political and economical fields was the Republic of China. For, whether needfully or not, Japan found it necessary to place conditions upon the maintenance of air transport arrangements with Taipei which Taipei could not possibly accept. That Peking found it possible to get the Japanese government to do this has to be chalked up as a major victory of Peking over Taipei in the political field. And no matter how the Republic of China and its flag carrier China Airlines make up for their losses in revenues from the Taiwan-Japan traffic, and no matter how they divert their carrying capacity into other uses, there is no escaping the fact that they could have done all those other things and still maintained their traffic to and from Japan unless the Peking regime had managed to get the Japanese government to cause its severance.

But the next attempt by Peking to get Japanese consent to their demand for exclusivity of privilege, in respect to shipping, has thus far failed. In the absence of a Peking-Tokyo agreement as to shipping relationships it is, of course, possible that shipping between the two countries can go on even though the Chinese Communists must put up with the situation of their ships being in the same harbors with ships flying the Nationalist flag. As of now, at least, that is what they must decide to do, unless they really want to keep their ships out of Japanese ports and forbid Japanese shipping from entering their harbors or their coastal waters.

What would this cost them? And if the economic costs were extremely heavy, would they decide to bear them because they knew they could rely upon the Japanese to eventually surrender? Much has been made of the Japanese success in getting Communist China to sell petroleum to Japan, up to two million tons a year in the near future, it is said. Could any such trade as this be carried in third-country bottoms? Possibly it could, but not very probably. Aside from the cost factor, one which would only deepen Japan's current problem of international payments, any such arrangements with third countries would at best be rather unstable and undependable. Much of the ongoing increase of production of oil in Communist China is dependent also upon foreign implementation, both technological and by way of actual supply, and it cannot soon be greatly magnified without both. The Peking policy of agreeing to oil exports to Japan must, therefore, be seen as largely a "come-on" to the Japanese, to entice them into a shipping transport agreement, no matter what the cost to them as to their currently most profitable trade with Taiwan. In light of the immediate background of air transport agreements, Tokyo-Taipei and Tokyo-Peking, it is very doubtful that the Japanese will in the shipping arrangements field be willing at all to sacrifice a real, even vital, economic interest of its own to the demands of Peking's political and economic warfare against Taipei.

The spectacular burgeoning of the trade between Japan and the Republic of China, it must be remembered, has taken place even under the conditions of the last two years when Tokyo has had diplomatic relations with Peking and not with Taipei. This is indeed a strong testimony as to the effectiveness of the new informal organizations for the conduct of relations between Japan and the ROC. And to keep things in proportion, the success of the ROC in this is a testimonial to the capability of its government to pursue the national aim of revolution and reconstruction in spite of and in the face of its loss of international prestige in other areas. The new informal organizations for the conduct of relations between the two countries have helped keep up the ever-increasing flow of persons and communications between them, so indispensable to their growing commercial relationships.

Thus as of this time there can be no verdict to the effect that the substantive relations between Japan and the ROC cannot and will not survive the rupture of their formal diplomatic relations, or that the new organizations set up to help operate the details of these substantive relations cannot do so. In respect to both their successes and failures in the support of the national interests of their respective countries, these new organizations have demonstrated their capability as arms of the national policies of their governments.

It is asserted by some people in both Japan and the Republic of China, as well as elsewhere, that this situation cannot continue, and that eventually the ROC must lose its political war with Peking. Therefore, they say, it will be both desirable and necessary for Taipei to declare its "independence" of "China" and take on a totally independent political status of its own. This, they say, will allow all third countries to enter into new diplomatic relations with this new political entity while at the same time enjoying full diplomatic relations with Peking.

Whether or not the Republic of China must lose out completely in its struggle with the Chinese Communists is a matter of opinion. But it is not opinion at all, but unarguable fact, that to neither Taipei nor Peking would any such so-called solution be an acceptable one. Both Peking and Taipei are absolutely adamant in their insistence that no third nation can simultaneously have full normal diplomatic relations with both the Chinese regimes. While some persons concerned with these matters in Japan are most firmly asserting that this "two Chinas" or "one China; one Taiwan" solution is the only feasible one, so that both these entities can have their own independent and secure existence, the Chinese Civil War still exists and the claims of both Peking and Taipei to legal sovereignty over the whole of China are still unresolved. While, to be sure, no one can well forecast the future very much in advance, this unresolved conflict seems to be a fixture for some time to come. In any normal policy-making future it would be folly to assume that this deep-rooted conflict is just simply going to "go away."

If this is the case, is there a case for the universal adoption among the powers of the Japanese formula, namely to have formal diplomatic relations with Peking and operate a large array of substantive relations with the ROC by non-diplomatic means such as those now existing between Taipei and Tokyo? The answer must be in the negative. The situation of Japan differs greatly, for example, from the situation of the United States. The latter power has, to a greater or less degree through time, not only the power to defend itself but power enough to influence international relationships and international security on a global basis. Its own security clearly requires that in the western Pacific, from Alaska down through southeast Asia, it must have a secure network of dependable military security arrangements. The same thing is required in the eastern Atlantic Ocean and in the Mediterranean. Thus, its current capability for moving in the direction of increasing as it can its substantive relationships with Communist China, requires on the other end of the Chinese spectrum the firm maintenance of its security arrangements with the Republic of China. As a prerequisite, it must continue its diplomatic relations with that government, for its treaty arrangements with it for mutual security in the military field could hardly survive the abrogation of its full diplomatic relations with Taipei. And to say this does not, of course, deny the full importance to both countries, both economically and politically, of the increasing trade, communication and cultural relations between the USA and the ROC.

Above all, for example, the Republic of China represents to the USA the most outstanding success, in all likelihood, in the whole world for our Foreign Aid policies since World War II. Are we going to just let all this go down the drain of history in favor of a wholesale and indiscriminate sell-out to Communist China, our main interest in which must, for a future of uncertain length, be in respect to playing the balance of power game between Communist China and the USSR? This is hardly conceivable. Particularly so since the best testimony we can get as to the intentions of Peking is that they are continuing to denounce the United States as "one of the two great imperialist powers," detente with which, they say, is based entirely upon their own self-interest. They are still highly chauvinistic and will cherish the modus vivendi between Peking and Washington only "as long as it is profitable to them." (Testimony of David K. E. Bruce, former head of the U. S. Liaison Mission in Peking before the Senate Foreign Relations Committee, *News from China,* 71 October 1974.)

Factors of this kind, especially when seen in conjunction with the obvious and inherent instabilities in the internal situation in Communist China, make absolutely mandatory for the foreseeable policy-making future a firm policy on the part of the United States of preserving and fostering its full program of relations with the Republic of China, diplomatic, economic, military and cultural. As long as the Chinese Communists want to develop relations with us in order to counteract possible Russian aggression against them, well and good. But we can never afford on that or any other account to abandon our firm, stable and prosperous relationship with the Republic of China which is a proven ally and a credit to the cause of modernization in Asia and the world.

APPENDIX

AGGREEMENT ON THE ESTABLISHMENT OF OFFICES IN JAPAN BY THE EAST ASIAN RELATIONS ASSOCIATION AND IN THE REPUBLIC OF CHINA BY THE INTER-CHANGE ASSOCIATION

Mr. Chang Yen-Tien and Mr. Koo Chen-Fu, representing the East Asian Relations Association (hereinafter called E.A.R.A.), and Mr. Teijo Horikoshi and Mr. Osamu Itagaki, representing the Inter-Change Association (hereinafter called I. C. A.),

Being desirous of facilitating their respective nationals, while residing or travelling in the territory of the other country, to enter, stay and educate their children; and of promoting, on people-to-people basis, the smooth development between the two peoples in the economic, commercial, technical and cultural fields and any other matters mutually related,

Have agreed to establish their espective offices in the territory of the other country, on the following terms:

I. The E.A.R.A. establishes an office in Tokyo and an office in Osaka. The Osaka office may set up a brance office in Fukuoka by despatching personnel there in long-term duty.

The I. C. A. establishes its offices both in Taipei and Kaohsiung.

II. The number of personnel either for the E.A.R.A. or for the I.C.A. in their respective offices shall be no more than thirty persons. Any increase of personnel as their business required shall be mutually agreed upon. The number of personnel mentioned above shall not include the assistants employed locally.

The two parties shall make sure that the necessary support, assistance and facilities, as their respective laws and regulations permit, be extended to the offices and personnel of each other.

III. The business and activities of the overseas offices of the two parties shall be limited to the following:

    (1) to contact and negotiate with the authorities concerned and to seek all necessary means for the purpose to render full protection

to, and to prevent from being injured, the persons, lifes and properties of their own nationals residing in the territory of the other party, as well as the rights, interests and properties of the juristic persons owned or established by their nationals in the territory of the other party;

(2) to engage in all matters with respect to the education of the children of the nationals of each party residing in the territory of the other party (including their overseas schools);

(3) to accord the necessary assistance to nationals of one party and nationals of any third country with respect to their entry into, taking residence in, and re-entry into the territory of the other party;

(4) to render all the necessary assistance with respect to the investigation or good offices in matters in which the nationals of the two parties are involved;

(5) to contact the authorities concerned and to seek the necessary means for the purpose to promote the trade between the two parties;

(6) to make survey on the economy, trade and tourism conditions of the other party and introduce them to their own country as an aid towards a balanced trade between the two parties;

(7) to conclude or assist in concluding various non-governmental agreements on trade, investment and technical cooperations between the two parties and to engage in all the necessary activities to assure their implementation;

(8) to engage in the necessary survey and contact with respect to the payments and repayments of loans involved in the previous Loan Agreements;

(9) to handle the business in connection with various technical cooperations between the two parties, including the implementation of the unfinished sections of the technical cooperation projects previously realized by international commitments;

(10) to render all the necessary assistance in order to ensure the safe operation for fishing boats of one party on the high seas off the sea shore of the other party;

(11) to render all the necessary assistance in order to ensure the safety of the ships of one party to enter or to leave the harbours and to operate in the harbours of the other party (including emergency

entry), and to assist the landing of the crew owing to the sickness, dismissal or other reasons.

The preceding paragraph concerning ships and their relevant business shall apply *mutatis mutandis* to aircraft;

(12) to contact and negotiate with the authorities concerned and to seek other necessary means for the purpose to maintain the smooth operations of the traffic of passengers and goods by air and by sea and other communications between the two parties;

(13) to seek all the necessary means to facilitate the inter-change between the two parties in academic, cultural and athletic activities;

(14) to engage in other necessary survey and relevant activities and to seek all necessary means in order to attain the goal as set forth in this Agreement.

The present Agreement is drawn up in the Chinese and Japanese languages.

IN WITNESS WHEREOF, the representatives of the two parties have signed the present Agreement at Taipei this twenty-sixth day of December, One Thousand Nine Hundred and Seventy-two.

For the representatives of the E.A.R.A.

(Signed)

For the representatives of the I.C.A.

(Signed)